SECOND EDITION

Test SUCCESS
in the
Brain-Compatible Classroom

*To our mothers, Closs Pickren Mizell and Louise Long Schaerer—
these dedicated teachers made a difference in the lives of
children and influenced us to become educators.*

*To all dedicated teachers and students in schools where
standardized tests are administered.*

*We present this book to make a difference in turning the test
scene into a learning celebration.*

SECOND EDITION

Test
SUCCESS

in the
Brain-Compatible
Classroom

Carolyn Chapman | Rita King

CORWIN
PRESS
A SAGE Company

For information:

Corwin Press
A SAGE Company
2455 Teller Road
Thousand Oaks, California 91320
www.corwinpress.com

SAGE Ltd.
1 Oliver's Yard
55 City Road
London EC1Y 1SP
United Kingdom

SAGE India Pvt. Ltd.
B 1/I 1 Mohan Cooperative
   Industrial Area
Mathura Road, New Delhi 110 044
India

SAGE Asia-Pacific Pte. Ltd.
33 Pekin Street #02-01
Far East Square
Singapore 048763

Printed in the United States of America.

Library of Congress Cataloging-in-Publication Data

Chapman, Carolyn.
Test success in the brain-compatible classroom/Carolyn Chapman and Rita King.—2nd ed.
      p. cm.
Includes bibliographical references and index.
ISBN 978-1-4129-6998-7 (cloth)
ISBN 978-1-4129-6999-4 (pbk.)
   1. Test-taking skills. 2. Test anxiety. 3. Students—Psychology. I. King, Rita M.
II. Title.

LB3060.57.C45 2009
371.26—dc22   2008030600

This book is printed on acid-free paper.

08   09   10   11   12   10   9   8   7   6   5   4   3   2   1

Acquisitions Editor:	Cathy Hernandez
Editorial Assistant:	Ena Rosen
Production Editor:	Libby Larson
Copy Editor:	Paula L. Fleming
Typesetter:	C&M Digitals (P) Ltd.
Proofreader:	Wendy Jo Dymond
Indexer:	Maria Sosnowski
Cover Designer:	Rose Storey

Contents

Foreword

The last 25 years can be characterized, at least in part, by efforts to improve America's public schools.

Unfortunately, while it is widely recognized that improved test results are the national measuring stick, there has been relatively little practical, research-based information available to teachers on how to help students improve their performance on these high-stakes tests. Aside from the obvious need for the effective teaching of significant content, are there additional ways teachers can help students improve their performance?

Carolyn Chapman and Rita King offer numerous specific, research-based suggestions in this book, *Test Success in the Brain-Compatible Classroom*. The premise of their work is that student success on tests is not accidental but the result of insight, planning, rehearsal, and preparation. This book contains ideas and suggestions that represent the best of both worlds, research and classroom experience. The book reflects the authors' deep understanding of the latest research and their many years of successful classroom teaching. Their goal is to transform the dreaded test day into a day of "celebration of the brain's phenomenal abilities."

Who can benefit from the book? Just about everyone—particularly school administrators, teachers, and parents. Readers will learn about such topics as ways of communicating content for ideal learning, memory strategies for retaining and retrieving more information, test-taking skills to integrate with all subjects, strategies to use with informal and formal tests throughout the year, techniques to teach individual test-taking habits, and ideas to create positive learning environments in the school and home. And there is much, much more.

Carolyn Chapman and Rita King have made it their mission to create a major paradigm shift regarding attitudes toward test taking. They call for a change in direction or, more specifically, a change in attitude—a change from negative to positive approaches to all tests. The ideas in this book will empower teachers, parents, and—most importantly—students to improve test performance.

—Dr. Robert Eaker

Dr. Robert Eaker, a professor and former dean in the College of Education at Middle Tennessee State University, consults with schools and districts nationwide on subjects such as school improvement and schools as learning communities.

Acknowledgments

Corwin Press gratefully acknowledges the contributions of the following reviewers:

Tamika Barrett
PhD Candidate in Education: Curriculum Design
University of Illinois at Chicago
Chicago, IL

Jolene Dockstader
Middle School English Teacher
Jerome School District #261
Jerome, ID

Tanya Marcinkewicz
Teacher
David W. Harlan Elementary School
Wilmington, DE

Ganna Maymind
Teacher
Asher Holmes Elementary School
Morganville, NJ

Sandra Moore
English Teacher
Coupeville High School
Coupeville, WA

Andrea Wardell
English Teacher
Eagle Ridge Middle School
Ashburn, VA

About the Authors

 **Carolyn Chapman** continues her life's goal to teach as an international educational consultant, author, and teacher of quality professional development opportunities. She supports educators in their process of change for today's students. Carolyn taught kindergarten-level to college-level classrooms. Her interactive, hands-on professional development opportunities focus on challenging the mind to ensure success for learners of all ages. All students *do* learn. Why not take control of that learning by putting excitement and quality into effective learning! Carolyn walks her walk and talks her talk to make a difference in the journey of learning in today's classrooms.

Carolyn authored *If the Shoe Fits . . . How to Develop Multiple Intelligences in the Classroom*. She coauthored *Differentiated Instructional Management: Work Smarter, Not Harder; Differentiated Instructional Strategies for Reading in the Content Areas; Differentiated Instructional Strategies for Writing in the Content Areas; Differentiated Instructional Strategies: One Size Doesn't Fit All; Test Success in the Brain-Compatible Classroom; Differentiated Assessment Strategies: One Tool Doesn't Fit All; Multiple Assessments for Multiple Intelligences;* and *Multiple Intelligences Centers and Projects*. Video Journal Inc. features Carolyn Chapman in *Differentiated Instruction*. Corwin Press multimedia kits featuring Carolyn include *Differentiated Instructional Strategies for Reading and Writing* and *Differentiated Instructional Management*. Carolyn's company, Creative Learning Connection Inc., offers a CD, *Carolyn Chapman's Making the Shoe Fit*.

These publications demonstrate Carolyn's desire and determination to make a positive impact on educators and students. She continues to write while teaching courses, conducting inservice trainings, giving keynote addresses at conferences, and working on-site in long-term relationships with schools and districts to provide professional development for educators worldwide. Contact Carolyn by calling (706) 597-0706, or via e-mail at cchapman@carolynchapman.com, or visit her Web site at www.carolynchapman.com.

Rita King, EdD, is an international trainer, keynote speaker, consultant, and author. She conducts training sessions for teachers, administrators, and parents. She served as the principal and director of the teacher-training program in Middle Tennessee State University's laboratory school. In this capacity, she taught methods courses and conducted demonstration lessons. Educators relate to Rita because of her background as a teacher and administrator and her experiences in PreK–12 classrooms. She has been recognized as an Exemplary Educator by the state of Tennessee.

Rita's doctorate degree is in educational leadership. Her undergraduate and doctoral studies were directly related to education and teacher training. The books Rita coauthored are best sellers. They include *Differentiated Instructional Management: Work Smarter, Not Harder; Differentiated Instructional Strategies for Reading in the Content Areas; Differentiated Instructional Strategies for Writing in the Content Areas; Differentiated Assessment Strategies: One Tool Doesn't Fit All;* and *Test Success in the Brain-Compatible Classroom.* Corwin Press multimedia kits featuring Rita include *Differentiated Instructional Strategies for Reading and Writing* and *Differentiated Instructional Management.* She coauthored training manuals for Creative Learning Connection's Train the Trainer courses.

Rita's sessions give educators and parents innovative, engaging activities to develop students as self-directed, independent learners. Her areas of expertise include differentiated instruction, classroom management, coaching, mentoring, brain-based learning, and test success. Participants enjoy Rita's practical, easy-to-use strategies; sense of humor; enthusiasm; and genuine desire to lead each learner to success. She may be reached by phone at (615) 848-8439, via e-mail at kingrs@bellsouth.net, or through the Web site for King Learning Associates Inc. at www.kinglearningassociates.com.

Introduction

The mind is not a vessel to be filled, but a fire to be kindled.

—Plutarch

TEST DAY . . .

. . . do these words lift your heart? Are your students ready with eager minds and sharpened pencils?

Probably not. We wrote this book to learn more about how the latest brain research can help us prepare students for optimal learning and standardized tests. We have witnessed the negative spirit in which tests are often administered and taken. Yet, as educators, we know students need positive learning to develop their knowledge of test-taking skills to succeed in school and beyond. These concerns about testing are based on our experiences in education, which include teaching and working in PreK through college classrooms. Our concerns also come from our work in consulting and assisting administrators, teachers, parents, and students with the standardized testing dilemmas. Our investigations and experiences lead us to call for a major paradigm shift from negative to positive approaches to all tests. Creating this change has become our mission.

Throughout this resource, you will find practical tips to design a brain-compatible classroom where every student can become test-ready. These ideas are drawn from our research and experiences involving optimal learning.

We know educators work diligently every day to meet the needs of each learner using differentiated instruction and authentic experiences. As a result, students are more self-directed and better problem solvers than in the past. However, students are not always able to show their abilities on tests. We believe teachers must create bridges between the many ways students learn and the way they approach formal test formats. The innovative learning strategies presented here are designed to teach students how to retain and transfer information to all tests, to all subjects, and to real-life experiences.

We believe everyone benefits when tests are viewed as celebrations of the brain's phenomenal abilities, not as dreaded events. To that end, this book is filled with practical ideas and suggestions for teachers, administrators, parents, and students to create positive test environments.

As "playwrights," we prepared this book to present the necessary tools to transform traumatic testing scenes into meaningful celebrations of learning. The stage is set for you. As the scenes unfold and you plan the performers' roles, we hope you will adapt the ideas and establish a positive climate where students tackle tests with the same high spirits they exhibit when approaching challenging games.

Join us in our preparation for the test performance . . .

—Carolyn and Rita

The Test Scene 1

All the world's a stage.

—William Shakespeare,
As You Like It (2.7.139)

THE CURRENT SCENE

Few students are able to avoid taking standardized tests. Currently, most state legislatures mandate annual standardized achievement tests in elementary, middle, and high schools. Reading, writing, math, science, and social studies are the most commonly tested subjects, though some states include spelling, health, and communication. It is the responsibility of school officials and classroom teachers to prepare for and administer these state-mandated tests.

Test scores are important to many people, especially educators. Teachers and administrators across the nation are held accountable for their students' test scores. The current trend is to make raises or merit pay dependent on the results. Many legislators and other decision makers believe educators work harder to increase achievement when they receive rewards for high scores or sanctions for low scores. Several states take control of schools in crisis with low test scores.

The public, too, is interested in test results. Newspapers and other media publish scores. Businesspeople analyze test results before locating a branch or a new company in a particular state, community, or school district. Real estate agents use test data to sell homes. In many instances, the public uses the scores as the sale criterion to judge the quality of teaching, schools, communities, and school districts. The leaders and the public want to know how schools are doing, and test scores provide a seemingly simple measure of success or failure, so standardized tests are here to stay.

IMPACT OF STANDARDIZED TESTING

Unfortunately, few students, educators or parents look forward to test days. Figure 1.1 outlines the impact testing has on students, administrators, teachers, and parents.

The wealth of knowledge acquired by students should be celebrated as a bright point in their educational experiences; too often, though, standardized tests place a dark cloud over the joy of learning. This doesn't have to be true. An appropriately staged test scene creates positive attitudes and successful experiences to foster the love of learning. We can

FIGURE 1.1	
Positive	**Negative**
Student Reactions	**Student Reactions**
Self-Efficacy I always do well. I am proud of myself. I showed what I learned.	Learned Helplessness I never do well. My classmates always score higher. There is no need for me to try to learn.
Teacher Reactions	**Teacher Reactions**

Empowered
 I prepared my students.
 My students knew how to apply
  test-taking skills.
 I am proud of our achievements.
	Defeated
	 My students' scores do not reflect their
	  growth.
	 I hate testing.
	 These students do not have a desire to
	  learn.

Administrator Reactions	**Administrator Reactions**

Elated
 My staff and the students
  took testing seriously and
  performed well.
 We are going to celebrate.
 In comparison to the other schools,
  we are one of the top schools.
	Frustrated
	 We have got to spend more time on
	  core content.
	 My faculty and the students have to
	  take testing more seriously.
	 Extracurricular activities have to be cut
	  out of our schedules.

Parent Reactions	**Parent Reactions**

Proud
 I am so proud of my child.
 I want my child to continue to go
  to this school.
 The teachers are doing a great job.
	Angry
	 Those teachers are not doing their job.
	 I need to move my child to another
	  school.
	 My child is smarter than the scores
	  reveal.

transform the nightmare of testing into a celebration of learning, if we prepare students for the test all year with intriguing, differentiated, brain-compatible strategies.

CHANGING THE SCENE: A PARADIGM SHIFT IN ATTITUDES TOWARD TESTING

Is there a learning experience that generates more anxiety than standardized testing? The term *test* holds deep-rooted, negative connotations for many teachers, administrators, and parents. These feelings easily transfer to students; they result in stress, fear of failure, memory blocks, and general anxiety. These emotional reactions interfere with learning.

In their article "Testing the Joy Out of Learning," Sharon Nichols and David Berliner (2008) highlight many ways high-stakes testing creates reluctant learners, as illustrated in the following statement: "From the motivation literature, we know that learners are more likely to enjoy learning when activities are meaningful, fun, or interesting. Yet, again and again, high-stakes testing diminishes the fun and meaning of learning" (pp. 14–15).

Most educators agree that the ultimate goal of education is to prepare students to pursue lifelong learning by awakening their desire to learn. Our goal is to help students learn test-taking skills through activities that are meaningful, enjoyable, and easily remembered. Effective teachers connect with students. They know what makes them "light up," and they know how to bring meaningful experiences to students' lives.

If students and teachers use tests as exciting, engaging challenges to show what was learned, we predict higher test scores and more rewarding learning experiences. This positive view of testing must be communicated to staff members and parents in a way that creates dissatisfaction with the "old" way of doing things and a new vision for change. The new ways must be internalized and become habits. This major shift to using a new perspective on the test-taking experience will require intensive training and a change in mind-set for everyone in the learning community.

SETTING THE STAGE FOR TESTING: A METAPHOR

We created the metaphor *setting the stage* to describe the process of preparing students and establishing appropriate learning environments for testing. The entire test-taking experience is compared to a Broadway production, from the first rehearsals to the final performance and the backstage cast party. You may find it helpful to use this theater metaphor with students,

FIGURE 1.2

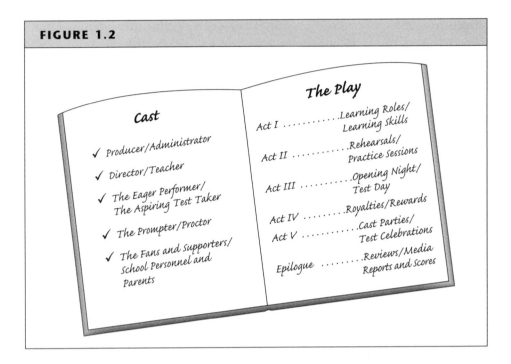

teachers, administrators, and parents as you introduce a positive view of testing. Enjoy the production!

THE CAST

The Producer: Administrator

On the Stage

The producer is in charge of all preparations for the performance. This individual oversees the personnel and coordinates the activities to create a success for everyone involved. A major role of the producer is to bring out the best in each crew member and performer to bring high acclaim to each individual and to the production.

In the School

The administrator oversees the teachers and staff, organizing and supervising throughout the preparations and test-taking experiences. A major role of the administrator is to create a learning environment and experiences that lead all learners to their potential. The goal of the effective administrator is to lead everyone to strive for high test scores in order to bring acclaim and success to students, the staff, and school.

The Director: Teacher

On the Stage

The director is a teacher, mediator, coach, and facilitator, selecting the play and making decisions about sets, rehearsal schedules, and pacing of scenes. A successful director motivates actors to be prepared and confident and to believe in the value of the material they are performing. A major role of the director is to guide and inspire cast members to give their best effort in each act.

In the Classroom

The teacher, like the director, must teach all required skills while keeping the atmosphere spirited on the testing journey. Through discussions and applications, the teacher must convince students that tests are valuable. The educator works diligently to teach the standards, skills, and concepts. Ongoing assessments are used to be sure students know, understand, and can apply the information. Students are prepared for tests by scheduling times to practice and explaining when, where, what, and how the tests will be given within the formal guidelines. The test director is responsible for maintaining a spirited assessment atmosphere while challenging students to achieve their best performance in each rehearsal and formal test.

The Eager Performer: The Aspiring Test-Taker

On the Stage

To be successful, actors must have a goal or internal driving force. This goal may be as simple as the desire to become a better performer. Most actors enjoy external rewards too—the attention of others, the sound of applause, the sight of their names in lights, and the accolades after the performance. But the best performance is given when the actor devotes heart and mind to the role.

In the Classroom

Students, too, must have the intrinsic desire to succeed on tests. This internal drive may be fueled by the prospect of reaching individual and group goals. Praise from teachers, administrators, and parents develops internal aspirations for test success. The best test performances occur when students combine knowledge, desire, and perseverance.

The Prompter: The Proctor

On the Stage

The prompter keeps actors focused on their lines, roles, and stage positions by standing in the wings ready to assist. A comfortable rapport needs to be established between the performers and this special assistant.

In the Classroom

A proctor is often assigned to a classroom to assist the teacher and the students during testing. The students can be very distracted by a proctor who is a stranger.

Administrators need to assign the person to the room early in the year. Periodically, this new person needs to teach the group, conduct observations, or talk to the class. The students need an explanation of this individual's role in the test scene. By doing this before the stressful test week, students become accustomed to the proctor's presence and voice.

The Fans and Supporters: The School Personnel and Parents

On the Stage

Individuals behind the scenes and in the community help make a production a success by supporting the performers. In stage performances, encouragement comes from the other actors in the production, stagehands, sponsors, theater owners, fans, friends, family members, and the audience.

In the Classroom

The administrators, teachers, specialists, support staff, custodians, and parents play their parts in encouraging and supporting students for test success.

PREPARING FOR AND PUTTING ON THE PRODUCTION

Learning Roles/Learning Skills

On the Stage

An actor must integrate all memorized lines and stage movements in order to appear natural in a character's role.

In the Classroom

Students must rehearse test-taking skills and strategies throughout the year with the content information and standards. The strategies must be integrated across the curriculum, through informal tests, and in daily work and life to make learning meaningful. When skills are internalized, they are easily and automatically applied during standardized tests, the most important performances of the year.

Rehearsals: Practice Sessions

On the Stage

The cast rehearses the performance over weeks or months. Finally, the director schedules dress rehearsals as formal practice sessions to simulate the actual performance. The performance is not interrupted for corrections or suggestions.

In the Classroom

Students practice test-taking skills all year. The final practice sessions before a major test are simulations of the main event, using the same formal rules. The formal practice sessions are administered with the same timing, atmosphere, environment, and directions established for the official test period. These rehearsals should be stimulating and challenging experiences.

Opening Night: Test Day

On the Stage

On opening night, excitement is in the air. Friends and family members wish the performers good luck. The stage is set. The crew is ready. The cast is anxious to begin. The director is prepared to signal the crew to raise the curtain.

In the Classroom

On the first day, or premiere, of the achievement test, an air of excitement is evident throughout the school and in the classroom. The performers are prepared and confident. This is a special time when the teacher and students cheer, "It's showtime!" and, "Let's show what we know!"

Royalties: Rewards

On the Stage

Amateur actors are rewarded with feelings of success and pride. Professional actors enjoy the same internal rewards, as well as salaries, which may come from a percentage of ticket sales.

In the Classroom

The immediate rewards for test takers include feelings of success and pride. Students also receive accolades from teachers, administrators, parents, and the community.

Cast Parties: Test Celebrations

On the Stage

After the performance, the cast and all involved in the production celebrate their success. This celebration often takes the form of an informal gathering, a formal dinner, or a backstage party. This is a time to say thank you and to congratulate everyone who made the performance a success.

In the Classroom

When tests are completed, students need and deserve a celebration. This event can be shared with parents, teachers, and administrators. Some suggestions for these special occasions include receptions, field days, free time, ice cream socials, pizza parties, pep rallies, or other special rewards enjoyed by everyone.

Reviews: Media Reports and Scores

On the Stage

When reviews are published, cast members use the feedback for encouragement and to improve their performances. If negative comments and criticism are pervasive and continue for a long time, actors may leave the production, or the show may close.

In the Classroom

Teachers, schools, and districts must withstand criticism and use it constructively. Parents and students may also receive feedback on the test data. Too much negative criticism leaves everyone feeling anxious or helpless. All data are used to improve teaching and learning.

THE AUTHORS' HOPE

We created this book as a valuable resource for you to set the stage for testing with a positive learning environment in the classroom, in the home, and throughout the school. The activities and strategies included incorporate the most recent research in brain-based learning. They are designed to provide educators and learners with a large repertoire of test-taking skills. We hope you use and adapt them as you prepare students emotionally, socially, physically, and academically for test day.

Testing—A Word 2 From the Experts

You've got to accentuate the positive, eliminate the negative.

—Johnny Mercer

RESEARCHING YOUR ROLE

In the theater, directors, set and costume designers, and actors conduct research as they prepare for a performance. We have done the same. The bibliography contains a complete list of the sources and references used in writing this book. Here is an annotated list of practitioners and researchers who shape our work related to learning and achieving test success in the brain-compatible classroom. We briefly identify key ideas from each expert and apply them to test preparation.

Caine, Renate Nummela; Caine, Geoffrey; McClintic, Carol; and Klimek, Karl

In their book *12 Brain/Mind Learning Principles in Action: Developing Executive Functions of the Human Brain* (2008), Renate Nummela Caine, Geoffrey Caine, Carol McClintic, and Karl Klimek present these brain/mind learning principles:

1. All learning is physiological.

2. The brain/mind is social.

3. The search for meaning is innate.

4. The search for meaning occurs through patterning.

5. Emotions are critical to patterning.

6. The brain/mind processes parts and wholes simultaneously.

7. Learning involves both focused attention and peripheral perception.

8. Learning always involves conscious and unconscious processes.

9. There are at least two approaches to memory: archiving isolated facts and skills or making sense of experience.

10. Learning is developmental.

11. Complex learning is enhanced by challenge and inhibited by threat associated with helplessness.

12. Each brain is uniquely organized.

Applications to Test Preparation

1. Create the learning and testing environment to meet the physical and social needs of each student.

2. Plan test preparation activities for the student's developmental stage and unique ways of learning.

3. Design engaging, meaningful experiences with instruction and test-taking skills to promote long-term memory.

4. Provide opportunities for students work together to learn and rehearse skills and strategies.

5. Strategically plan instruction to focus attention. Constantly be aware that everything in the student's peripheral vision effects learning.

6. Teach skills and strategies in the unique ways individual students learn.

7. Provide time for students to process test-taking skills and strategies thoroughly by embedding them in lessons throughout the year.

Costa, Art

Art Costa (2007) is a renowned champion for the teaching of thinking. His phrase "home for the mind" reflects the strong belief that students must have exciting and challenging places to learn. He believes schools should teach processes for thoughtful learning, so students become independent thinkers. Costa's list of intelligent behaviors that are characteristic of independent thinkers includes the following:

- Persistence and risk taking
- Decreased impulsivity
- Metacognition
- Striving for accuracy
- Drawing on past knowledge and applying it to new situations
- Employing different strategies to learn (See Chapter 3 for suggestions for fostering intelligent behaviors in the test scene.)

Applications to Test Preparation

- Teach students how to "keep on keeping on" and to make a reasonable guess if the rules and time permit.
- Emphasize and rehearse thoroughness and accuracy in daily tasks and routine tests. For example, see activities associated with "bubbling in" in the section of this title in Chapter 7.
- Teach and model specific strategies to "think about thinking." See Chapter 8 for many strategies students can use to think about their thinking when taking a test.
- Bridge prior experiences and new learning to create mental connections.
- Involve various senses in test preparation experiences to help place information and strategies in long-term memory.

Csikszentmihalyi, Mihaly

Csikszentmihalyi (1990) studied the state of "flow," a deep sense of pleasure that accompanies optimal learning experiences. For the most beneficial learning to occur, experiences must be inviting, stimulating, and interesting. Hobbies, sports, intriguing games, and favorite pastimes bring participants into the state of flow. Intrinsic rewards and self-esteem accompany such activities. According to Csikszentmihalyi, the state of flow occurs when

- there is no fear of failure,
- there are clear goals,
- the rewards of accomplishment are felt,
- there is no boredom or frustration, and
- the mind is challenged.

Applications to Test Preparation

- Provide a test-taking environment that encourages risk taking.
- Clarify purposes and objectives for learning test-taking skills and strategies. See the "Purpose" sections of Chapter 7 and the "Beyond the Classroom Doors" sections of Chapter 8.
- Design experiences for task success.
- Match activities with students' abilities and interests.
- Use pleasant test-taking experiences that invite and challenge learners. See Chapters 6, 7, and 8 for ideas on creating pleasant, stimulating environments and experiences.

Diamond, Marian

Diamond, a neuron anatomy professor, analyzed the effects of the environment on the brains of rats. She found enriched environments to be conducive to producing connections between nerve cells, with an increase in intelligence. Diamond coauthored *Magic Trees of the Mind: How to Nurture Your Child's Intelligence, Creativity, and Healthy Emotions From Birth Through Adolescence* (1999). She advocates the creation of classroom cultures that have the following characteristics:

- Enriched learning environment
- An atmosphere free of undue pressure and stress combined with pleasurable intensity
- Emotional support for learners
- Emphasis on nutritious diets.
- Activities that meet mental, physical, aesthetic, social, and emotional needs
- Experiences that stimulate the senses

Applications to Test Preparation

- Establish learning environments that offer a myriad of experiences.
- Encourage student choice in activities.
- Choose experiences that reflect the enjoyment of learning.
- Share activities related to good nutrition.
- Provide appropriate, challenging, test-related activities.
- Consider individual students' needs when test-related activities are designed.

Feuerstein, Reuven

Reuven Feuerstein's work is described in *Mediated Learning: Teaching Tasks and Tools to Unlock Cognitive Potential* (Mentis, Dunn-Bernstein, &

Mentis, 2008). Feuerstein analyzed the impact of cultural deprivation on intelligence. He provided opportunities for low-functioning students to apply what they learned and witnessed an increase in their intelligence. His work stressed the value of matching approaches to individual student needs, the interpersonal relationship of the teacher and learner, and the role of encouragement in learning. Feuerstein's studies contradicted the belief that intelligence is fixed. He was not interested in what students learned but how they learned. His work shows

- the right conditions for learning should be established,
- the teacher–learner relationship influences learning,
- approaches should match learner needs, and
- all students can learn.

Applications to Test Preparation

- Build strong teacher-pupil bonds to enhance learning.
- Remove the barriers to test success, including negative attitudes, fear, and anxiety. (See Chapters 1, 6, and 9.)
- Be a facilitator of independent thinking. (See Chapter 5.)
- Demonstrate through actions and words the belief that all students can learn.
- Promote test-taking experiences as opportunities to learn and increase intelligence.

Gardner, Howard

In his book *Frames of Mind* (1983), Howard Gardner presents his theory of multiple intelligences, which evolved during a ten-year study of cognitive development in children. His findings, presented in the first edition of the book, supported Feuerstein's theory that intelligence is not fixed. We address eight of Gardner's intelligences, which identify the many ways individuals learn, think, and solve problems. The intelligences are verbal/linguistic, musical/rhythmic, visual/spatial, logical/mathematical, bodily/kinesthetic, naturalist, interpersonal, and intrapersonal. His ideas affect learning in classrooms where educators use the many ways students learn as a guide to teaching. Key elements include the following:

- Everyone has at least eight intelligences.
- Everyone's brain is unique.
- Most individuals have three or four areas of strength among their intelligences.
- Weaker intelligences can be strengthened if desire and interest are combined with positive experiences.

Applications to Test Preparation

- Engage students' strong intelligence areas to teach test-taking skills and strategies.
- Design experiences to activate the intelligences.
- Enhance storage and retrieval of information for test success with challenging, exciting experiences.
- Teach students to transfer the many ways they learn to test formats. Most tests target two intelligences: verbal/linguistic and logical/mathematical (as discussed in depth in Chapman, 1993).

Goleman, Daniel

Goleman's (2006) book *Emotional Intelligence: Why It Can Matter More Than IQ* is filled with information about the impact of emotions on learning. Goleman advises schools to teach students how to identify and control their emotions, emphasizing that the ability to learn is directly affected by emotions. He envisions educational programs that include the development of self-awareness, self-control, empathy, listening skills, conflict resolution, and cooperation.

Goleman's work emphasizes the importance of

- controlling impulses and moods;
- knowing strategies to control depression, anxiety, and anger to optimize memory skills;
- being able to cheer yourself up when feeling down; and
- learning to be optimistic.

Applications to Test Preparation

- Remove barriers to thinking such as worry, frustration, fear, and nervousness.
- Provide experiences that teach students to identify their negative and positive reactions to tests.
- Teach strategies to decrease negative reactions and enhance positive reactions.
- Provide parents with information and guides related to the role of emotions in test success.

Gregorc, Anthony

Gregorc, author of *The Mind Styles Model: Theory, Principles, and Practice* (2006), developed the Mind Styles Model of learning styles or preferences. He describes these styles as follows:

- Concrete/random: Independent, risk-taking, experiential learner
- Concrete/sequential: Organized, factual, efficient, task-oriented, detailed learner
- Abstract/sequential: Intellectual, analytical, theoretical, critical, convergent learner
- Abstract/random: Imaginative, emotional, interpretative, holistic, flexible learner

Applications to Test Preparation

- Vary instruction to reach more students. (See Chapter 4.)
- Align strategies for teaching test-taking skills with the learning styles of individual students.
- Be aware that pencil-and-paper practice sessions are not the best way for most students to prepare for a test.
- Maximize student potential by planning individual and small-group activities.
- Devote class time to teaching students about their individual thinking processes.
- Design lessons that move students from concrete, sequential activities to more abstract and random experiences.

Jensen, Eric

Eric Jensen is the author of numerous books related to the brain and learning. Here are some key points from his synopsis of brain research in *Brain-Based Learning* (2008):

- Growth of new brain cells is enhanced by exercise, lower levels of stress, and good nutrition.
- Social conditions influence our brain in ways we didn't know before.
- The brain has the ability to rewire and remap itself.
- Chronic stress is a very real issue in schools for both staff and students.
- What we eat has an effect on cognition, memory, attention, stress, and intelligence.
- Exercise is strongly correlated with increased brain mass, better cognition, mood regulation, and new cell production.
- Environments alter our brains.

Application to Test Preparation

- Intersperse exercise before and between test segments to enhance thinking. Provide outdoor exercise, if possible.

- Identify and eliminate stress producers related to testing for students, staff members, and parents.
- Emphasize the value of nutrition on learning and memory for test success.
- Provide opportunities for students to interact.
- Strategically design a positive testing environment and experiences for optimal brain functioning.
- Keep in mind that each student's brain is altered by each learning experience.
- Plan to lead each individual to his or her potential with feedback from test preparation activities.

Perkins, David

Perkins, author of *Outsmarting IQ: The Emerging Science of Learnable Intelligence* (1995), states that teachers should teach thinking skills explicitly using a thinking vocabulary. Prepare students for situations with simulated activities and events. Use new knowledge in a different setting to enhance retention and retrieval.

Applications to Test Preparation

- Apply thinking skills to test preparation activities. Instruct students in thinking skills to transfer learning to test formats and to all areas of learning, including everyday activities.
- Show students how to analyze their thought processes during test practice sessions.
- Establish a critical-thinking classroom with an emphasis on transferring relevant content to real-life situations.
- Teach students to be proficient in "self-talk" to enhance their thinking processes.
- Provide activities that simulate the testing scenario.

Sousa, David

In his book *How the Brain Learns* (2006), David Sousa presents practical ways for educators to understand and apply recent discoveries related to the brain. These findings include the following:

- The brain continually uses a process called neuroplasticity to reorganize itself on the basis of input.
- Emotions affect learning, memory, and recall.

- The brain seeks novelty. Humor, movement, multisensory instruction, quiz games, and music can be used to place novelty in lessons.
- The brain is better prepared for tests following two minutes of exercise and two ounces of fruit (dry fruit is recommended) followed by eight ounces of water.

Application to Test Preparation

- Be aware that each experience changes the brain's wiring.
- Provide an emotionally safe learning/testing environment.
- Use novelty to intrigue the brain and enhance memory. Remember that test anxiety is relieved by adding touches of humor to drill and practice sessions.
- Provide opportunities for students to move before tests and between test segments.
- Engage the learner's various senses in instruction to create memory pathways.
- Use game formats to rehearse facts, skills, concepts, and test-taking strategies.
- Give students opportunities to place facts and skills in a familiar melody or rhythm.
- Provide healthy snacks, especially fruit and water, before tests.

Sprenger, Marilee

Memory expert, Marilee Sprenger, applies the latest research on learning and the brain in strategies, practical ideas, and techniques to enhance memory skills. In *Memory 101 for Educators* (2006), she uses the acronym N.E.V.E.R. F.O.R.G.E.T. as a mnemonic to present the memory strategies.

Application to Test Preparation

Adapt and apply each component of the N.E.V.E.R. F.O.R.G.E.T. acronym to enhance learning and prepare your students for tests.

Notice: Train the brain to focus on the information or task.

Emote: Create emotional ties for learning experience.

Visualize: Teach students how to use the "mind's eye."

Exercise and Eat Right: Infuse physical activity and nutrition habits.

Rest: Emphasize the brain's need for sleep to process information.

Free Yourself of Stress: Use relaxation and exercise activities.

Organize: Teach strategies to plot, list, sequence, and categorize.

Rehearse: Practice with a variety of strategies and formal rehearsals.

Guard Your Brain: Teach students ways to protect the brain.

Enrich Your Brain: Use new, intriguing, challenging activities.

Teach: Provide learners opportunities to share knowledge and skills.

Sternberg, Robert

Sternberg advocates broad measures of intelligence. In *Successful Intelligence: How Practical and Creative Intelligence Determine Success in Life* (1996), he identifies analytical, creative, and practical abilities as three aspects of intelligence. Among an individual's analytical abilities is the ability to evaluate. The creative aspect of intelligence includes the ability to create, design, brainstorm, invent, and use the imagination. The practical aspect of intelligence is knowing how to apply what one knows. Individuals' strengths in these three intelligences vary.

Applications to Test Preparation

- Help students learn to use analytical intelligence in evaluating each possible answer to find the correct response.
- Plan activities that use the creative aspect of intelligence to retain and retrieve content.
- Design instruction involving the three aspects of intelligence.
- Apply test-taking skills to life outside the classroom so practical learners understand the test's purpose and the experiences become more meaningful.

Sylwester, Robert

Robert Sylwester's book *How to Explain a Brain: An Educator's Handbook of Brain Terms and Cognitive Processes* (2005) is recommended for anyone interested in creating a brain-compatible classroom. He presents information used in the cognitive neurosciences in terms all educators can understand and apply to enhance learning and assessment.

The following excerpts are from Sylwester's valuable resource:

- Amygdala: The amygdala is "a paired complex of structures the shape and size of an almond that recognize innate biological fears and activate relevant primal automatic responses. . . . [It] is located in the lower frontal areas of the two temporal lobes." This emotional control center "adds positive and negative emotional content to the memory of an experience" (p. 18).

- Endorphin: This is a "commonly used term for a class of peptides discovered in 1973 that reduce intense pain and enhance euphoria" (p. 65).
- Mirror neurons: These are "neurons in the premotor cortex and possibly elsewhere that activate when observing a specific action in another person (such as a smile) and also when carrying out the same action" (pp. 103–104).
- Nutrition: "Although our brain encompasses only 2% of our body's weight, it uses 20% of all our nutrient energy" (p. 123).
- Play and games: "The recent reductions in school arts programs and an atmosphere of play are . . . a biological tragedy that we'll come to regret when our society matures in its understanding of our brain's developmental and maintenance needs" (p. 132).

Applications to Test Preparation

- Use multisensory techniques to teach and practice test-taking strategies.
- Engage students in exercise and interpersonal activities to provide pleasant experiences related to testing.
- Model or demonstrate test-taking skills and strategies to activate mental mimicry and enhance memory.
- Emphasize the value of nutritious meals and snacks to feed the brain.
- Design test preparation activities with play and game formats to intrigue the mind.

Brain experts continue to add to the vast world of knowledge related to how the brain functions. All educators need to be aware of the most recent research on how the mind understands and retains information to design learning environments and instruction for test success.

The Test-Taking Cast

3

Behavior is a mirror in which everyone displays his own image.

—Goethe

Every successful director develops a repertoire of strategies and habits to help performers achieve their best when the curtain rises. You can do the same for your cast of test takers so each student becomes test-ready for the best possible performance.

Before students reach your classroom, they have learned a variety of attitudes and behaviors, good and bad, related to testing. Some will be excited, ready to show what they know. Others will be nervous, distracted, or disruptive. As the testing director, you transform established, ingrained negative feelings into more positive ones.

The idiosyncrasies and general behaviors of students are obvious to teachers during the first few weeks of school. Your observations of student reactions to chapter, unit, and weekly tests provide a guide for initial interventions and/or praising affirmations. Identify each learner's habits, attitudes, behaviors, characteristics, and reactions to tests so you can assist them in improving their approaches to all test experiences.

CHARACTERS IN THE TESTING SCENE: WHO'S TESTING WHOM?

Although each student is unique, students tend to share observable characteristics when faced with the phrase "Take out a number-two pencil." Just as plays and films have characters, the classroom has a unique cast. Most teachers recognize the following test-taking characters. We provide a description of each character with an "Intervention Suggestions" list to deal with test-taking behaviors that hinder quality performance. The following characters are found in all grade levels.

Blurting Blake

Blurting Blake has a habit of disrupting the classroom. This tendency needs to be corrected right away. A student with this habit wants to control all conversation in the room and be the center of attention. Often, this learner is so focused on a particular question or topic that the teacher's additional comments and directions are missed.

Observed Behaviors and Attitudes

- Yells out comments and questions.
- Interrupts.
- Disturbs others by talking out loud.
- Raises hand and talks at the same time.
- Mumbles comments.
- Likes to hear own voice.
- Points out the errors of others.
- Needs to read information aloud to comprehend.
- Makes disruptive, distracting noises.
- Other _____

Intervention Suggestions

- Establish and enforce the rules.
- Praise appropriate behavior.
- Use proximity. Stand or sit near the student.
- Teach respect for peers.
- Indicate how the behavior affects others.
- Explain how easily concentration is lost.

- Teach self-monitoring techniques. For example, show the student how to use a timer, self-check list, or journal.
- Provide avenues for quick feedback through checklists or teacher notes and verbal statements with specific comments.
- Other _____

Cheating Charlie

Cheating Charlie frustrates classmates and is resented by students who follow the rules. Cheating occurs when the learner does not know the answer or is unsure about answers. A student may cheat simply because cheating has brought success. Whatever the cause, early detection and correction eliminate or reduce later trouble.

Observed Behaviors and Attitudes

- Sits in view of a classmate's test.
- Places cheat notes in a sock, sleeve, or desk.
- Writes answers on hand or on a note.
- Leans out of chair toward classmates.
- Walks near classmates' desks during tests.
- Other _____

Intervention Suggestions

- Preserve the student's dignity.
- Correct the behavior in private.
- Remove the student from the group quietly.
- Conference.
- Use cover sheets.
- Use proximity. Stand or sit near the student.
- Use good touches, such as a hand on the shoulder.
- Use eyes and nonverbal cues.
- Review consequences during practice sessions.
- Seat the student in a study carrel.
- Other _____

Clock-Watching Cleo

Clock-Watching Cleo is so channeled into the timing of the test that it hinders performance. This learner is usually a perfectionist who wants to be sure there is time to do the task correctly. The clock watching becomes obsessive. Often, this student does not understand how much can be accomplished in a period of time. Assist the learner using timed tests throughout the year.

Observed Behaviors and Attitudes

- Looks at the clock constantly.
- Waits, pencil poised, for the test to begin.
- Rushes through the test.
- Appears anxious to begin.
- Does not listen to directions.
- Demonstrates careless work.
- Other _____

Intervention Suggestions

- Place a watch or small clock on the student's desk to teach the student how to work with timed segments.
- Use timed games and tests throughout the year.
- Explain time constraints thoroughly.
- Teach self-pacing strategies.
- Use timed activities in routine activities and assignments.
- Other _____

Crying Crystal

Crying Crystal displays unusual emotions as the assessment date approaches. For this student, tears flow at highly stressful, frustrating times, such as tests.

Observed Behaviors and Attitudes

- Cries during tests.
- Exhibits nervous tension such as nail biting, twisting the hair, drumming a pencil, or twitching movements.
- Shows emotional outbursts in pressured situations.
- Becomes highly sensitive.
- Sniffles, whimpers, and disturbs others.
- Other _____

Intervention Suggestions

- Eliminate the possibility of medical or serious emotional problems.
- Give the student a stuffed animal to cuddle.

- Ignore the behavior if it is not disturbing others or interfering with learning.
- Give warm smiles, words of comfort, and understanding pats on the back.
- Encourage the student to walk around, wash his or her face, or stretch during transitions.
- Other _____

Don't-Care Danny

Don't-Care Danny appears to tune everything out. However, this attitude may be deceptive, because the student is usually capable of learning more. The student with this behavior must be stimulated, challenged, and intrigued to tune in. Sometimes this behavior occurs because it has been accepted for a long time. Be aware that other underlying problems may create this bad attitude, such as peer rejection, learned helplessness, fear of the unknown, and lack of knowledge.

Observed Behaviors and Attitudes

- Displays off-task behavior.
- Plays with toys or objects.
- Exhibits an "I don't care" attitude.
- Sees no purpose in testing.
- Gains attention by not working.
- Focuses on everything but testing.
- Other _____

Intervention Suggestions

- Give rationale for testing throughout the year.
- Hold individual conferences regularly.
- Use a game format to teach test-taking skills.
- Use a World Series, playoff, or other relevant metaphor for testing.
- Give the student responsibilities, such as assisting the teacher.
- Provide opportunities for the learner to coach weaker students.
- Provide enticements and rewards.
- Other _____

Sleepy Selena

Sleepy Selena needs a good night's sleep. Rest is necessary for physical preparedness in all learning. When a student is sleepy, nodding and dozing is apparent. However, sleepiness may be an escape mechanism to cover feelings of low self-esteem.

Observed Behaviors and Attitudes

- Demonstrates tiredness.
- Whines constantly.
- Keeps head on desk.
- Appears dazed and lethargic.
- Appears to be in another world.
- Covers head with an article of clothing.
- Drools on the test booklet
- Other _____

Intervention Suggestions

- Check for medication and/or physical problems.
- Provide physical activity before and after test sections and learning segments.
- Ask about the amount of sleep obtained.
- Monitor room temperature. Warmth makes individuals sleepy.
- Use good touches, handshakes, pats on the back.
- Allow the student to get some fresh air.
- Use proximity. Stand or sit near the student.
- Assign responsibilities, such as passing out papers.
- Give time for a drink of water.
- Provide manipulatives.
- Other _____

Twiddling Tim

Twiddling Tim's continuous movement or twiddling may be a nervous, anxious habit. Early identification of these behaviors will alert you to the need for interventions such as gentle reminders, one-on-one chats, and/or formal instruction. On the other hand, excessive body movement may simply be this student's way to keep mental juices flowing. The learner's brain may need the physical stimulation to transmit mental messages efficiently and to concentrate.

Observed Behaviors and Attitudes

- Wiggling
- Shuffling feet

- Rocking in chair
- Lifting desk with knees
- Playing with objects in desk
- Fidgeting
- Twisting strands of hair
- Moving leg constantly
- Biting nails
- Other _____

Intervention Suggestions

- Ignore! Ignore! Ignore the behavior, if it is not disturbing other learners or interfering with teaching.
- Use one-on-one instruction.
- Let the student use manipulatives.
- Find the student an isolated work area.
- Provide extra energy outlets during transition periods.
- Other _____

Hung-Up Harry

Hung-Up Harry gets stuck on information that he does not know and then refuses to move on. A student with this behavior often expects adults to provide the answers. This learner may shut down entirely with the task and show signs of high frustration.

Observed Behaviors and Attitudes

- Looks for peer assistance.
- Chews pencil.
- Whispers.
- Appears stumped or lost.
- Continuously raises hand to solicit help.
- Quits when the answer is not found immediately.
- Lacks confidence.
- Other _____

Intervention Suggestions

- Encourage the learner to skip unknown words and to look for clues.
- Teach the student to use first inclination—the first answer considered is often right.
- Explain that no student is expected to get all answers correct.

- Encourage the student to answer easy questions first.
- Model and show the student how to use self-talk, such as "Try it," and "Give it your best shot."
- Teach the student to skip the question and come back to it later, if time allows.
- Other _____

Sick Sam

Sick Sam becomes physically ill in stressful situations. The pupil with these behaviors may also fake illness or talk himself into being sick to avoid a test. The mental pressure causes emotional and physical reactions. This student should have to make up all work to prevent sickness from becoming its own reward.

Observed Behaviors and Attitudes

- Doesn't want to come to school.
- Becomes sick before coming to school or before tests.
- Experiences stress-related headaches or stomachaches.
- Becomes physically ill at school.
- Faints or appears pale.
- Other _____

Intervention Suggestions

- Identify possible physical or emotional problems.
- Provide positive, successful test-taking experiences throughout the year.
- Give parents tips to relieve the student's anxiety.
- Let the student take the test in the most comfortable position.
- Talk to parents early in the year about the learner's unusual reactions to tests.
- Acknowledge the learner's feelings but don't dwell on them.
- Other _____

Ready Richie

Ready Richie is mentally, physically, and academically prepared for the test. This learner is comfortable in the learning and testing environment. He is confident about the content knowledge, has mastered the test-taking skills, and is able to transfer what is known to the test. Ready Richie is the model test taker.

Observed Behaviors and Attitudes

- Bright eyed and bushy tailed
- Focused on the task at hand
- In ready mode with materials and thoughts
- Confident
- Prepared and eager to face the challenge of a test
- Other _____

Intervention Suggestions

- Call on the student to model test-taking strategies and skills.
- Ask the student to write, model, and share his or her "smart talk" or self-talk used during testing.
- Ask the student to explain personal approaches to testing situations.
- Challenge the student to explore new test-taking strategies.
- Other _____

Tolerant Teacher

Reflect on the student's behavior before taking a corrective action. You may be the only individual in the room disturbed by it. Analyze test-taking behaviors that seem to be intolerable. For instance, most teachers insist that everyone sit upright in their seats during tests. Consider permitting students to take tests in a more natural, relaxed position.

Questions to Ask When Observing Behaviors

- Is the behavior contrary to classroom or school rules?
- Is it helping the student?
- Can you and the other students ignore the unusual body position, movement, or other behavior?
- Will intervention interrupt the concentration of other students?
- Would a correction interfere with this student's performance?
- Is the behavior disturbing other students?
- Is the behavior tolerable?
- Other _____

Intervention Suggestions

Reflect on the class as a whole. Ask yourself which behaviors really prevent students from working up to their potential. Consider how you can help them learn better habits. Over time, teach the whole class appropriate test-taking behaviors on formal and informal assessments.

- Assist students in recognizing and understanding unacceptable behavior.
- Brainstorm acceptable alternatives to replace the negative behavior.
- Have students verbalize proper behavior.
- Ask students to identify a peer model.
- Have successful older students share their experiences.
- Create and use a Behavior Improvement Action Plan. (See instructions in Figure 3.1.)
- Other _____

FIGURE 3.1

Behavior Improvement Action Plan

When a student's behavior disturbs or distracts another student or interferes with performance, the behavior needs to be corrected. Follow these suggested steps:

1. Describe the behavior in detail. What are the unique, observable traits that need correcting? This detail can help you to interpret and analyze the real problem.

2. Document instances of the behavior. Record dates and times. Look for patterns. Does the behavior occur at a specific time of day, during a specific type of activity, on the same day of the week?

3. Write a detailed, step-by-step plan for improvement. Explain what changes need to occur and by a specific date. If possible, involve the student in creating the plan.

4. Share the plan with the student and/or parent. Include expectations.

5. If a negative behavior persists, involve parents with improvement goals.

PLAYING THE IDEAL ROLE

It is wise to remember that students are individuals; many of them have distracting habits. If a particular behavior neither interferes with the student's learning nor bothers peers, ignore it. If it is a problem, work with the student toward improvement.

Learning to play the ideal role, like Ready Richie, is just one skill students and performers must master to do their best on the big day. They also must learn how to remember and deliver their lines. Memory, a key performance skill, is the subject of the next chapter.

> *Our evolving mission compels us to embrace a new vision of assessment that can tap the wellspring of confidence, motivation, and learning potential that resides within every student.*
>
> —Rick Stiggins

Memory in 4
Action

Learning the Part

Without memory we vanish, we cease to exist, our past is wiped out and yet we pay little attention to it except when it fails us. We do precious little to exercise it, to build it up, to protect it.

—Mark Twain

BUILDING MEMORY

In theater, the crew builds a set with carefully selected key props to help the audience imagine a particular scene. In a similar way, we construct our sense of events in our past out of bits and pieces of memory, filling in the context with general knowledge.

If the props are too vague or too few, we are unable to imagine the scene being performed on stage. If the "bits and pieces" to construct a memory are too vague or few, our memory fails.

A student's brain pays attention when a teacher provides information the learner needs or which connects to prior experiences. When this occurs, the brain is activated for the information to travel to short-term or long-term memory.

Too often, critical information ends its excursion in short-term memory because no connections are made. Short-term memory is used to deal with the immediate situation. For example, when a new telephone number is used immediately and forgotten, it passed through short-term memory. It is no longer needed, and the information journey has ended. Short-term or working memory usually lasts no more than a few seconds (Sprenger, 1999).

When information is rehearsed in unique, meaningful ways, connected to prior experiences, and used often, it will take its place in long-term memory. A friend's telephone number will enter long-term memory because it is needed and used often. The information will be held in long-term memory until it is needed again. For information to move into long-term memory, it must be used by the learner and rehearsed in unique, personal, and meaningful ways for easy retrieval. When students understand and know how to apply memory strategies, they will be better able to retrieve skills and information needed during tests.

MEMORY STRATEGIES: HELPING STUDENTS LEARN THEIR PARTS

The ultimate goal of teachers is to give each student a knowledge base for a productive and prosperous life. The goal is not to see how many facts can be retained in memory for tests. What is of primary importance is learning how to learn in order to learn and understand more (Gill, 1993). Students take tests throughout their education so it is imperative that they have a thorough understanding of test-taking skills and know how to apply them. To accomplish this daunting task, students must have an understanding of how learning takes place and a thorough knowledge of their personal ways of learning. Memory-control strategies prepare learners to be confident as they approach tests and related experiences.

Mnemonic Devices

Use what talent you possess: The woods would be very silent if no birds sang except those that sang best.

—Henry Van Dyke

Mneme (nay-may), a Greek word, is closely related to the English word memory. A mnemonic device is an aid for remembering facts, numbers, names, and ideas for easy recall. Teachers and parents often note that it is easy for children to remember games, jokes, goofy sayings, riddles, plots of movies, and anything they are told NOT to remember. That is because these bits of information come with "hooks"-memory tricks and unusual, vivid connections to prior learning that help learners store information and ideas. Students who apply mnemonic tools as props to build memory improve their test performance.

The following activities, tips, and strategies teach students how to remember facts using visual, verbal, rhythmic/musical, and bodily/kinesthetic devices, as well as other memory triggers. Many strategies presented here are from ancient memory specialists. Other suggestions are more recent, including those based on the multiple intelligences in Figure 4.1. You will find it easy to adapt these fun-filled strategies to teach students how to remember facts and transfer knowledge to formal test formats.

Remember the Facts Poem

To remember a fact you need to know
Sing it, move it, or see it as you go.
If you need just one more way
Write it, draw it, or act it out one day.
This will ham up your acts
To recall awesome facts!

USING VISUAL DEVICES TO IMPROVE MEMORY

We often say that someone with excellent recall has a "photographic memory." Visual memory is very powerful. Visual memory techniques can and should be taught in many ways and throughout the curriculum. The information provided here will get you started.

Visualization

Seeing pictures in one's mind is an excellent tool to remember information. Students need to be taught how to awaken and control this memory device. We have included a variety of tips for teaching students to use visualization as a memory tool or hook that leads to future learning.

Open the mind's eye. Students should sit quietly and comfortably. Begin the visualization by talking the class into a picture. Some verbal cues to begin a visualization include

- Visualize this . . .
- Picture this . . .
- Recall that . . .
- Think of a time when . . .

Don't mention the eyes. When picturing images in the mind's eye, people do not usually close their eyes. When you read a novel, you do not close your eyes to picture an exciting scene—the pictures appear in

FIGURE 4.1

Actions for Learning and Retaining Information

Verbal/Linguistic	Musical/ Rhythmic	Logical/ Mathematical	Bodily/ Kinesthetic
Read it.	Create a rhythm.	Make a pattern.	Act it out.
Spell it.	Rap it.	Chart it.	Feel it.
Write it.	Make a cheer.	Sequence it.	Be it.
Listen to it.	Create a jingle.	Create a mnemonic.	Role-play.
Recall it.	Hum it.	Analyze it using technology.	Simulate it.
Use your words.	Identify sounds.	Think critically.	Manipulate it.
Apply it.	React to sounds.	Use numbers.	Explore it.
Chunk information.	Listen to sounds.	Prove it.	Experience it.
Say it.	Connect to music.	Interpret the data.	Take a field trip.
Discuss it.	Write a poem.	Use the statistics.	Live it.
Connect ideas.	Create a chart.		Move body.

Visual/Spatial	Naturalist	Intrapersonal	Interpersonal
Color code it.	Label it.	Use self-talk.	Talk face-to-face with someone.
Highlight it.	Categorize it.	Work independently.	Bounce ideas around with someone.
Shape a word.	Identify it.	Solve it your own way.	Have empathy.
Interpret a graphic.	Form a hypothesis.	Understand self.	Listen to others.
Read a chart.	Conduct an experiment in nature.	Journal it.	Solve it together.
Study illustrations.	Adapt it.	Rehearse it.	Work in cooperative groups.
Visualize it.	Relate it to nature.	Use prior knowledge.	Talk on the telephone.
Make a chart.	Improve the environment.	Make your own links.	Write letters, blogs, or e-mail.
Create a poster.	Study conservation of water or energy.	Connect it.	
Use graphic organizers.			
Construct a replica.			

your mind. Yet, when a classroom teacher directs a group to picture something or recall information, often one of the first things said is, "Close your eyes. Now think of a time . . ."

Use short wait time. An image is captured quickly in the mind's eye. For this reason, television advertisements flash rapidly from image to image.

Talk it! After students capture the image in the mind's eye, give them the opportunity to turn to a partner and describe the image.

Describe it! Not everyone pictures things the same way. Tell students to use adjectives to describe details of the image in the mind's eye.

Use it! After a visualization, you can bridge to another activity, such as reading, writing, or science. For instance, after class members picture how their home state looked a long time ago and share their images, segue into a lesson comparing contemporary and pioneer homes. Visualization techniques can "hook" a current lesson to previously taught material, using phrases like these:

- Recall last week when we were . . .
- Picture the character who . . .
- Think back step by step . . .
- Picture that time in your mind . . .

Do it! Build in opportunities for students to use visual imagery. Emphasize its purpose as a learning tool for life.

Imagery Slates

An imagery slate is a technique that consists of mentally projecting an image onto a blank surface or imaginary slate. Each participant, including the teacher, needs a blank surface for the slate, such as a table or desktop, floor, chalkboard, or piece of paper. Talk through the targeted information while the students mentally draw an outline of the shape or plot the data on the slate. This procedure fixes the picture in their minds. Tell students to "rerun the picture in your mind" or "rewind your VCR and tell me what you did." Use this technique whenever students need to learn a new procedure or to process information for comprehension.

Activity: State Map

1. Ask students to think of the map of their state.

2. Model how to visualize and draw the imaginary shape of the state with your finger on your slate.

3. Establish top, bottom, right, and left, as well as north, south, east, and west. Students point to the location/direction on their imaginary slates as you name it.

4. Name cities, geographic landmarks, and other famous sites one by one.

5. Monitor and assess the students' knowledge as they draw and point on their own flat surfaces.

6. Check accuracy by referring to the wall map or a reference book.

Graphic Organizers: An Overview

Graphic organizers are pictures and shapes that organize and convey information in an immediate, memorable, visual form. For example an organizer in the shape of a spider can help students categorize what they know about an issue, separating fact from opinion. See Figure 4.2 for the sample organizer. Imagine your class is discussing a controversial issue, removing a soda machine from the school's cafeteria. Each student should record the topic, such as "Soda machine in high school cafeteria," in the spider's head. Known facts, such as "The money from the machine is used to buy computer equipment," are written in the spider's body. The learner records personal opinions such as "A little soda doesn't hurt" on the spider's left legs. The student listens to and writes down other opinions such as "Schools shouldn't sell unhealthy foods" on the spider's right legs. Possible actions such as "Remove it?" or "Keep it?" are recorded on the spider's antennae, if appropriate. Finally, the student states a conclusion, such as "The value of the machine does not outweigh the cons," next to the spider.

Tips for Teaching Students to Use Graphic Organizers

- **Teach by example and repetition.** Plot information on an organizer routinely in different classroom situations. When you model the use of organizers in several lessons, students see how they work.
- **Show how a specific organizer can represent a particular logical relationship.** By using the same graphic organizer in many different situations, learners see how it works in varied applications. For example, use a spider organizer to show students how to separate facts from opinions in language arts, social studies, science, and other subjects.
- **Vary organizers.** Students become bored when an organizer is overused. If you hear "Oh, no! Not another mind map!" then it is time to use another organizer that serves the purpose and entices the learner.
- **Encourage students to adapt organizers in their own ways.** Let students play with the designs. A funnel is a great tool to help students focus their ideas about a topic (funneling ideas into a conclusion). Some pupils may use this same organizer for another purpose.
- **Encourage students to use organizers independently.** Teach them to invent their own graphic organizers in various shapes—animals, cars, clouds—to fit the material to be learned.
- **Model how to create new graphic organizers.** For example, a class of kindergarten students visited a Civil War home that was decorated for the Christmas season. When the children returned to their classroom,

FIGURE 4.2

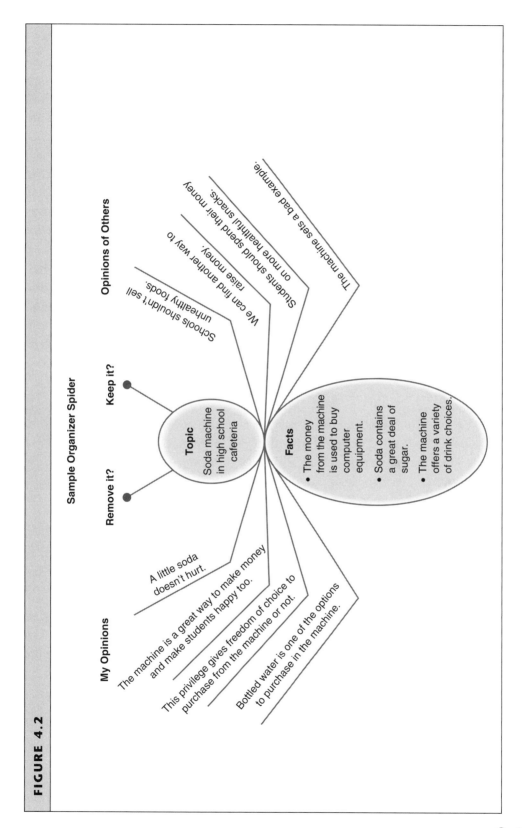

Sample Organizer Spider

Opinions of Others

The machine sets a bad example.

Students should spend their money on more healthful snacks.

We can find another way to raise money.

Schools shouldn't sell unhealthy foods.

Keep it?

Remove it?

Topic
Soda machine in high school cafeteria

Facts
- The money from the machine is used to buy computer equipment.
- Soda contains a great deal of sugar.
- The machine offers a variety of drink choices.

My Opinions

A little soda doesn't hurt.

The machine is a great way to make money and make students happy too.

This privilege gives freedom of choice to purchase from the machine or not.

Bottled water is one of the options to purchase in the machine.

FIGURE 4.3

their teacher designed a Venn diagram with a Christmas tree intersecting an outline of a typical home and the period home they had visited. This visual stimulated thinking about the many ways the two homes were alike (comparison). The students' brainstormed responses were written on the Christmas tree. Older students could also write specific characteristics beside each home to illustrate contrasts. (Idea contributed by Linda Vile, elementary teacher.)

Activity: Language Experience

After the teacher models how to use various organizers several times, students are ready to begin inventing their own. Use this exercise after a new experience, such as a field trip or science experiment, to allow students to practice designing graphic organizers. This activity is called a language experience.

1. Shortly after a class experience such as a field trip, ask students, "What design should we use to represent our experience today?" For example, if the class attended a basketball game, the students might decide to represent the experience by drawing the outline of two players to compare and contrast the two teams.
2. Have students supply the details to fill in the design.
3. Write student responses on the board, chart, or overhead. Use the students' exact words and their design suggestions.

Note: Younger students may use a shape that is familiar because you have modeled it. Older students should be able to invent original designs to suit the experience.

Picture Organizers

Pictures make great organizers. In the Graphic Organizer Collection on pages 45 and 46, we include some unusual ones for your reference, as well as some sample activities using picture organizers. Adapt these organizers, or even traditional ones like Venn diagrams, to your content.

Activity: Using Venn Diagrams

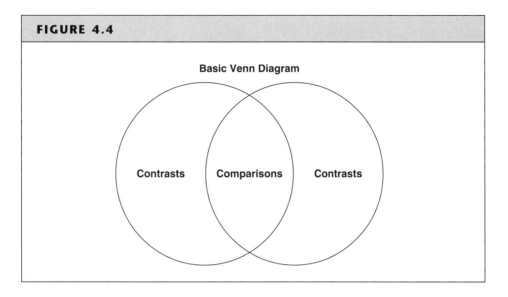

FIGURE 4.4

Basic Venn Diagram

Contrasts   Comparisons   Contrasts

Basic Venn Diagram

Venn diagrams are charts or graphic organizers that represent the compare-and-contrast relationship. The most basic form of a Venn diagram consists of two overlapping circles, each labeled with an item to be compared. In the middle, where the circles overlap, students write things the items have in common. In the sections of the circles that don't overlap, students write contrasts. Teach students to use a variety of Venn diagram forms throughout the year. Let students have fun with them. Items to compare and contrast include plants, cultures, planets, sports, regions, books, chemical compounds, games, geometric shapes, characters, musical instruments, and vehicles.

An introductory activity using an adapted Venn diagram is "My Friend and I . . ." See Figure 4.5 on page 44. This exercise is especially effective when students do not know each other well. Follow these steps:

1. Pair students.

2. Have each pair draw two overlapping circles on a piece of paper. Each circle represents one student in the pair—student A or student B. Student A's name is placed under one circle, and student B's name under the other circle.

3. Students can personalize the circles by drawing in their own features and clothing, such as hair, eyes, nose, mouth, ears, collars, and hats.

4. Students interview each other to identify hobbies and favorite things.

5. Students record ways they are alike in the overlapping part of the circles. Examples include: We both—like to sing, have three brothers, have two cats.

6. Students record the ways they are different in the outer parts of the circles. Student A might record "I am from Oregon" on one side, while Student B writes "I am from Florida" on the other side.

FIGURE 4.5

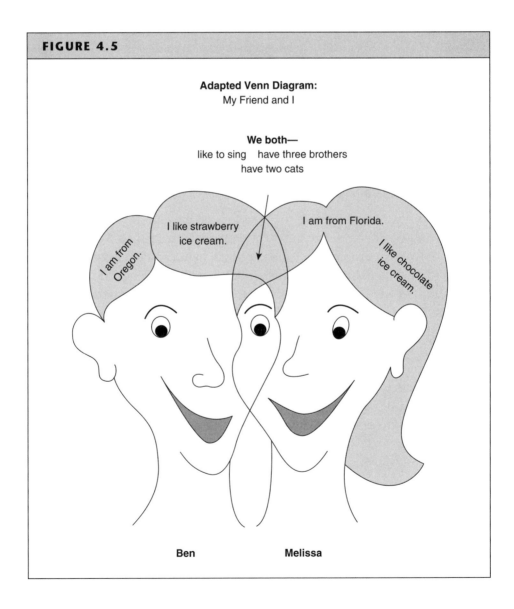

Adapted Venn Diagram:
My Friend and I

We both—
like to sing   have three brothers
have two cats

I like strawberry ice cream.

I am from Florida.

I am from Oregon.

I like chocolate ice cream.

Ben   **Melissa**

FIGURE 4.6

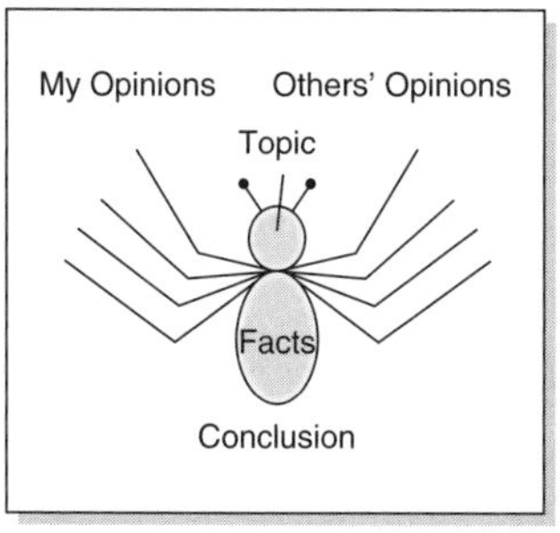

My Opinions   Others' Opinions
Topic
Facts
Conclusion

Spider

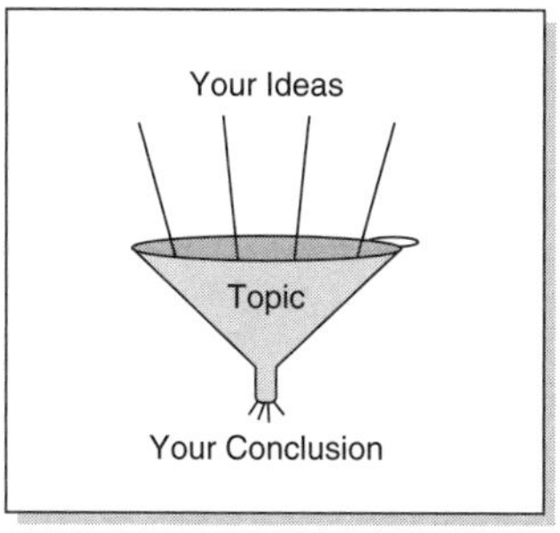

Your Ideas
Topic
Your Conclusion

Funnel

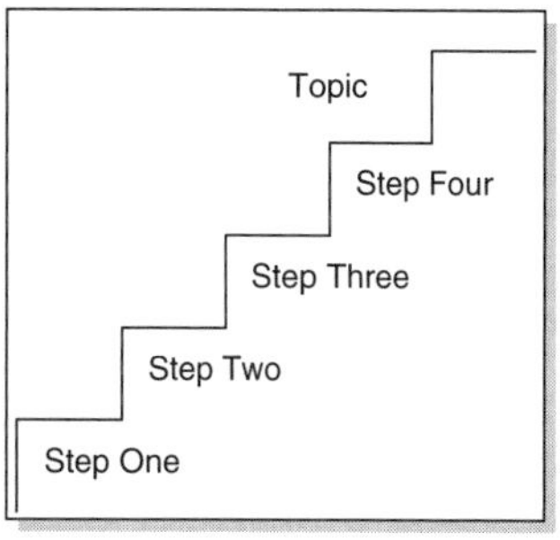

Topic
Step Four
Step Three
Step Two
Step One

Steps

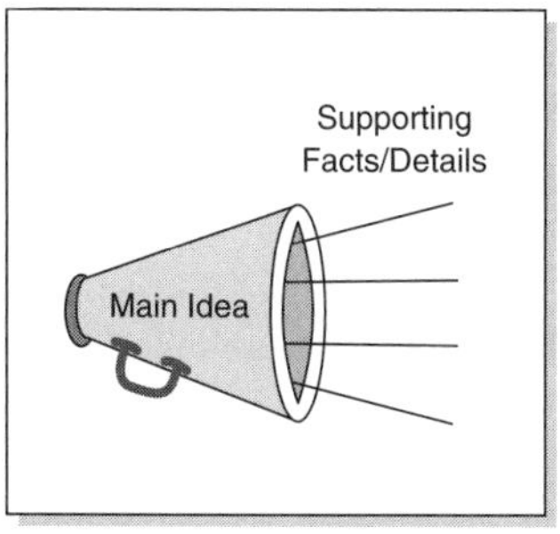

Supporting
Facts/Details
Main Idea

Megaphone

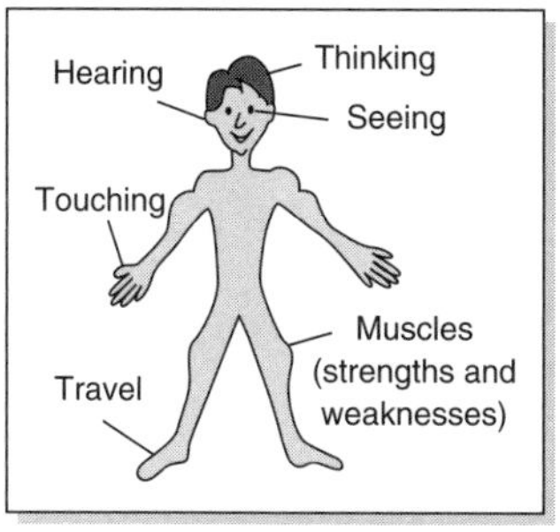

Hearing   Thinking
            Seeing
Touching
            Muscles
            (strengths and
Travel   weaknesses)

Character Sketch

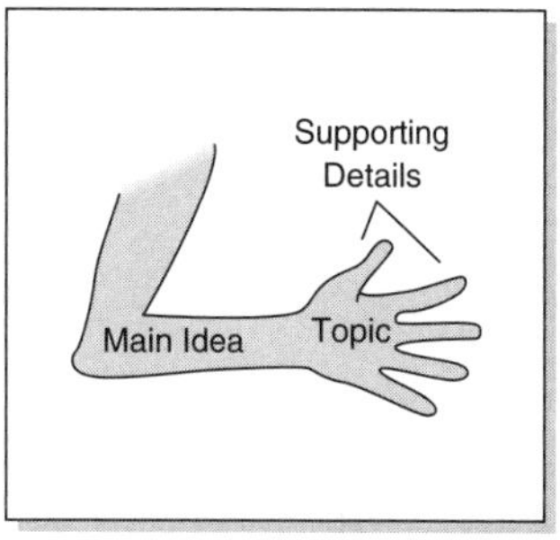

Supporting
Details
Main Idea   Topic

Arm and Hand

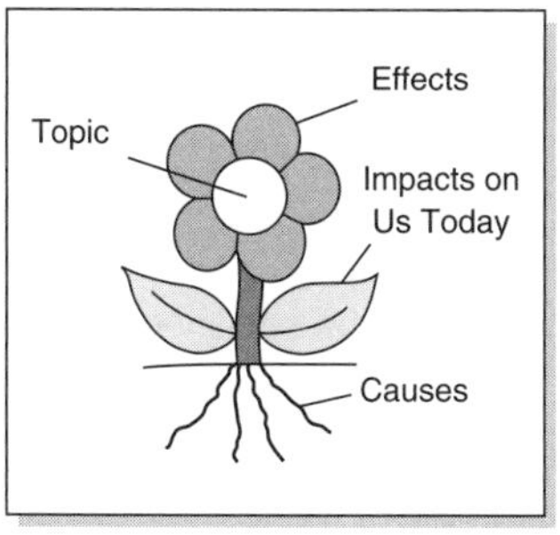

Effects
Topic
Impacts on
Us Today
Causes

Flower

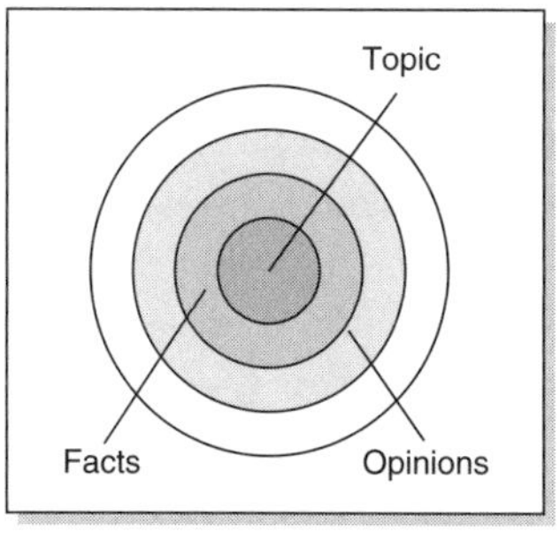

Topic
Facts   Opinions

Target

What   What
Happened   Happened
Next?   Last?

What   Then
Happened   What
First?   Happened?

Train

FIGURE 4.7

Graphic Organizer Collection Key

Spider

Separates facts from opinions.

Directions: Write topic on head, facts in body, own opinions on left legs, others' opinions on right legs, and conclusion below or next to spider.

Example: Organize facts and opinions in a debate about moving a soda machine from a high school cafeteria.

Funnel

Funnels ideas to the conclusion.

Directions: Write topic on a funnel. Write your ideas on lines flowing into the funnel. Place your conclusion at the end of funnel.

Example: Funnel ideas to a conclusion about the best ball player of the 20th century.

Steps

Outline a process.

Directions: Write the topic on the top step; starting on the bottom, write a key word/phrase to signify a phase in the process on each step.

Examples: Show how a computer is assembled or the steps in a science experiment.

Megaphone

Shows how to support a main idea or topic with facts/details.

Directions: Write the main idea on the megaphone and facts/details on lines coming out of the megaphone.

Example: Support the main idea in a paragraph about the motives of a character with details from the story.

Character Sketch

Inspires discussion of the attributes or experience of a historical figure or character.

Directions: Write what the figure or character hears, thinks, sees, and touches in appropriate places. Write places this person has traveled near the feet. List strengths and weaknesses near the muscles. Add a heart and list feelings.

Example: Fill in with experiences Abraham Lincoln had during his childhood to bring this historical figure to life.

Arm and Hand

Show how to support a main idea or topic with facts/details.

Directions: Write the topic on the palm, the main idea on the arm, and supporting details on the fingers.

Example: See "Megaphone."

Flower

Shows cause and effect.

Directions: Write the topic in the center of the bloom and the causes on the roots. Write impacts on us today on the stem and leaves; write effects on petals.

Example: Show the causes, effects, and impacts of World War II on us today.

Target

Shows how to zero in on the topic.

Directions: Write the topic in the bull's-eye, the facts in the adjoining circle, and opinions in the outer circle.

Example: Zero in on the causes of pollution.

Train

Shows a series of events.

Directions: Write what happened first on the first car, what happened second on the next car, and so on to the last car (what happened last).

Example: Identify the sequence of events in a passage.

FIGURE 4.8

Thinking Boxes

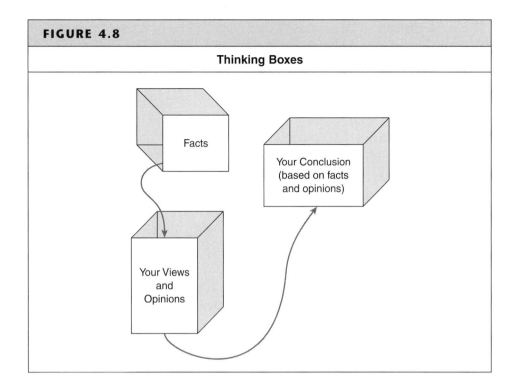

Thinking Boxes

Teach students how to use Thinking Boxes to organize ideas and information. Abstract thinkers and older students, in particular, may find these "visual outlines" useful.

G.O. Dozen

Graphic organizers are memory tools that may be used before, during or after instruction. If students have little or no experience in using organizers, model each one before using it in as an assignment. The following suggestions and tips for using graphic organizers can be adapted to any subject or grade level.

- Use a design or outline of an object in the content lesson to create the graphic organizer. The visual will make it easier for students to recall the information.
- Display an organizer that grows with the topic of study. Add information in each lesson to make it an on-going collection of important facts. For example, hang a long, wide ribbon and attach one or more facts on index cards daily.
- Use an organizer as a homework assignment for students to gather information from the reading of a content assignment.
- Use a timeline as an assignment for events or procedures. If time permits, tell students to illustrate it with mini pictures or symbols.

- Ask students to draw a stick person to represent an important figure or character in the lesson and fill in the attributes.
- Show students how to use bold dark colors to write the main ideas or most important facts with thin lines and lighter colors for the supporting details.
- Write the most important information in large print with the details in smaller print.
- Use different colors to highlight similar facts.
- Add texture to organizers using wallpaper, scraps of material, glitter, ribbon and yarn.
- Use similar shapes to depict specific groups or categories. For example, during a science lesson on atoms, write proton facts in triangles, neutron facts in squares and electron facts in circles.
- Create three dimensional organizers. Connect boxes, containers or objects with ribbon, rope or yarn. Attach pictures and words as labels.
- Vary the way organizers are used to add novelty to lessons. Assign them for independent, partner or group work. Use them as focus activities, for brainstorming sessions, to collect information during a class assignment, as a review or a test.

Using Graphic Organizers to Interpret Data

On a test, students are often asked to interpret data on a chart or graph. To prepare, students must work to interpret and understand plotted data throughout the year. Try some of the following ideas to help get them ready.

- Have cooperative groups plot information on a graphic organizer. Share the graphic to allow the class to interpret the information. This exercise gives students practice in using graphics to communicate information.
- Let students work independently and plot data, without using the text, and share their results. This exercise will demonstrate what they know and their needs.
- Ask students to use the text to gather more information to add to the organizer. Tell them to find a partner and share this information. This facilitates independent learning.
- As an extra step at the end of the exercises above, prepare multiple-choice questions using the information on the graphic. Design your questions to target both explicit and implicit thinking. Students practice using the chart to look up information (explicit thinking), and manipulate information to find answers (implicit thinking). Place your sample questions on a transparency, whiteboard, or computer screen for everyone to see. After students record their answers, ask them to share their thinking process—why did they dismiss answers A, C, and D, but choose B? Demonstrate the best way to approach each test item.

Color Coding

Choose a series of eight colors and use them as a color-coding system throughout the year. A color series might be black, red, blue, green, brown, orange, purple, and pink. The most important tip for success with this approach is to establish and maintain the eight-color series in all tasks. This can involve the whole school, so everywhere students go they see and use the same color sequence. Here are a few ways to use color coding in your classroom.

- Syllables. The first syllable in a word is black, the second red, the third blue.
- Directions. Color code directions to be followed in a center, project, math procedure, recipe, work station, lab, or assembly line.
- Procedural Order. Write each step in a different color or have a colored dot, number, or check beside it. For example, step one is black, step two is red, step three is blue, step four is green, and so on.

Example of Using Color in Procedural Order:
Steps in Long Division

1. divide (black)

2. answer (red)

3. multiply (blue)

4. subtract (green)

5. bring down (brown)

6. go back up (orange)

7. remainder (purple)

8. check (pink)

Variation: Put the steps in long division to a beat (Divide . . . bring down!).

Drawing Associations

A well-known mnemonic is one that links information with locations, including parts of the human body and other "places" (activity adapted from Turkington, 1996).

Activity: Drawing a Supply List

In this activity, students incorporate a supply list into a drawing of a person. They learn to associate information with location using pictures they create.

1. Visualize the following supply list projected onto an image of your principal. Remember, the more outrageous the placement of the objects, the easier it will be to recall the items.
   - Notebook . . . forming a hat on the principal's head.
   - Pencil sticking through the hat.
   - Ruler forming a tie for the principal.
   - Lunch money . . . on his shirt.
2. Draw the sequence and share the results.
3. Recall the list by visualizing the character.

Variations: Students place information on other locations or designs, such as the classroom or their own homes.

MEMORY IN ACTION: USING WORDS TO IMPROVE MEMORY

For individuals with strong verbal skills, often the easiest way to remember information is to link it to words or letters. All students, however, benefit from learning these verbal memory-control techniques.

Acronyms

Acronyms are new words, nonsense syllables, or phrases formed from the initial letters of the words in a series or list, as in the following examples. The acronym may be used to memorize lists, to remember steps, or to recall directions.

Examples of Acronyms	
ROY G BIV	Colors of the Rainbow: Red, Orange, Yellow, Green, Blue, Indigo, Violet
Scuba	Self-contained Underwater Breathing Apparatus
NATO	North Atlantic Treaty Organization
Laser	Light Amplification by Stimulated Emission of Radiation
HOMES	Great Lakes: Huron, Ontario, Michigan, Erie, Superior

Activity: Roy G Biv

Draw Roy G Biv (acronym for the colors of the rainbow) with red hair, orange bow tie, yellow shirt, green suspenders, blue pants, indigo socks, and violet shoes.

Acrostics

An acrostic uses the first letter of each word in a phrase or list of words to form a name, motto, message, or silly saying.

Sample Acrostics	
Planets	Many Vigorous Earth Men Jump Straight Up to Neptune (Mars, Venus, Earth, Mercury, Jupiter, Saturn, Uranus, Neptune)
Treble Clef Notes	Every Good Boy Does Fine

Activity: Acrostics Galore

1. Practice using a few sequenced alphabet letters to form a phrase.

    All Boys Can Draw

    Each Fat Grasshopper Hopped

2. Have students write an acrostic with "kind" words (adjectives) to describe a classmate, teacher, parent, or friend, based on that person's name.

    Beautiful

    Energetic

    Trusting

    Helpful

Activity: Acrostic in the Library

Challenge students to make an acrostic for the Dewey Decimal System.

000   General Works

100   Philosophy

200   Religion

300   Social Science

400   Philology

500   Natural Science

600   Useful Arts

700   Fine Arts

800   Literature

900   History

USING RHYTHM AND SONG TO IMPROVE MEMORY

Creating a rhythm for important bits of information is an effective, fun way to learn, store, and retain information. Create songs, poems, jingles, raps, chants, and cheers to teach concepts and facts.

Rhyme It!

Rhymes are familiar, effective ways to enhance memory for specific information. See the following examples:

- *I* before *E* except after *C*.
- Multiply! Times sign. Divide! Division line.
- Thirty days has September, April, June, and November. . . .

Sing It!

Most English-speaking children learn the alphabet song, "Abcdefg . . . now I know my ABCs," early in their school careers or before. Make up your own teaching songs. Take a concept that is difficult to teach and put it to a beat. Here are some ideas to get you started.

Activity: Spelling With a Memory Beat

1. Any word that has three to seven letters will fit in the tune of "B-I-N-G-O." Sing "B-I-N-G-O, B-I-N-G-O, and Bingo was his name-O." Now watch all the color words fit: R-E-D, R-E-D, R-E-D, R-E-D, R-E-D, R-E-D, and red is our color. P-U-R-P-L-E, P-U-R-P-L-E, P-U-R-P-L-E, and purple is my color.

2. Any word with eight or more letters fits the Mickey Mouse Club theme song: M-i-c-k-e-y M-o-u-s-e, C-h-r-i-s-t-o-p-h-e-r, g-e-o-g-r-a-p-h-y

Activity: Rhyming Words

Teach a specific skill with a song. In this example, the song verses teach rhyming words.

"Did You Ever See?" from Carolyn Chapman's *Making the Shoe Fit,* written by Carolyn Chapman

Did you ever see a giraffe laugh?
Did you ever see a giraffe laugh?
Did you ever, ever, ever?

No, I never, never, never
No, I never saw a giraffe laugh.

Variations: Did you ever see a . . . goat float; snail sail; frog jog; shark bark; cat bat; fox box?

Activity: Silent Hum

Practice this activity with your students when they need to master bits of information. Adapt the following dialogue to teach these steps.

1. Identify for yourself what you need to remember: a list, definition, or steps in a procedure.

2. Hum (silently to yourself) the information to a beat to create a rhythmic association. Use the beat of a famous song or jingle, or one of your own invention.

3. Create a musical hook to remember what you need to know. When you need to recall it, hum it to yourself.

Rap It! Cheer It!

Students also benefit from using quick, high-energy raps and cheers to recall information.

Activity: Number Rap

Create or ask students to create raps like this one as memory tools.

Number Line Rap

12345 hopping on up the line
That is when we use the addition sign.
54321 move on way back
It's a fact! Here we subtract!

Activity: Number Cheers

Students are familiar with cheers used at sporting events. Ask them to create information cheers like these examples using numbers.

Symbol Cheer

Addition! Plus sign,
Subtraction! Minus line,

Multiply! Times sign,
Divide! Division line.

Even and Odd Cheer

Two, four, six, eight
Even numbers are great!
One, three, five, seven, nine
Odd numbers are so fine!

USING THE BODY AND MOTIONS TO IMPROVE MEMORY

Riding a bicycle is a skill you never forget. The most fundamental way to know something is to remember it with actions. Get students into the habit of acting out ideas with their bodies by showing some examples. Allow time for students to develop their own motions. Use body-knowledge strategies throughout the year while teaching difficult concepts. Students will have fun learning and remember the information, too.

Acting Out Concepts

Most adults can remember and play the "This little piggy went to market" game—the memory exists right in our toes, so to speak. Students who map ideas onto their own bodies with movement fix the learning into long-term memory. Movement activities can be used in different content areas. They are especially useful to teach information learners need to access rapidly throughout life. The sample activities that follow can be adapted in many ways.

Activity: The Food Pyramid (Health)

Food Pyramid: A Poem

Eat three ounces of whole grains three times a day
Add green and orange veggies all along the way.

Fruit is a healthy snack for you to eat.
Fat-free/low-fat calcium can't be beat.

Include meat or fish that is lean
With bean, peas, or nuts for protein.

Be active for sixty minutes every day
You'll stay slim and trim living this healthy way!

The Food Pyramid in Motion

1. Show the interactive food pyramid from the Web site of the U.S. Department of Agriculture. Discuss the details of each food group.

2. Divide the students into the following groups: (a) grains, (b) vegetables, (c) fruit, (d) milk or calcium-rich food, (e) meat and beans, and (f) physical activity.

3. Challenge the students to create a five-minute presentation in motion for the class that will teach the information with everyone joining in the actions.

Presentation choices:

Role play	Rap
Carousel	Chant
Dance	Mingle Jingle
Cheer	

Activity: Parts of a Letter (Language Arts)

Bodily motion can be used as a valuable tool for retaining information. In the following activity, students associate the parts of a letter with parts of the body using motion.

Heading:	Point to your head.
Greeting:	Make a smiley face at your mouth.
Body:	Move both hands from your shoulders down to the top of your legs.
Closing:	Bend your knees and point to them with both of your hands.
Signature:	Point to your shoe. It probably has a special brand name or signature.

Activity: How Blood Flows Through the Heart (Science)

This activity helps students remember a process through movement.

1. Form a capital A with two fingers on your right hand. A stands for atrium. Say, "Right atrium, blood from the body."

2. Form a V with your right hand. V stands for ventricle. Say, "Right ventricle."

3. Cross your arms over your chest, saying, "Blood flows through lungs."

4. Form an A with your left hand, saying, "Left atrium."

5. Form a V with your left hand, saying, "Left ventricle."

6. Throw your arms out in front of you, saying, "Out to the body! That is the way the blood flows to the heart."

Activity: Macarena Multiplication (Mathematics)

This activity links multiplication facts to a dance, the macarena. Adapt other dances to sets of facts and procedures.

1. Instruct students who know the macarena to go to the front of the room. Most of the class will go to the front of the room. Students can demonstrate or teach each other the moves, if necessary.

2. Display the answers to the times tables (1–12), each on a separate strip of poster board. For example, display the six times table (6, 12, 18, 24, 30, 36, 42, 48, 54, 60, 66, and 72) on one strip of poster board.

3. Tell the class you are going to work on a particular number set—for example, the six times table. Tell them that each number from the set will have a motion of the macarena pattern. In the case of the six times table, start with 6 (6 x 1 = 6) with your right arm in front of you, hand facing the floor. Then call for 12 (6 x 2 = 12) with your left arm in front of you, facing the floor. Then call for 18 (6 x 3 = 18) with your right arm out and hand up, and so on.

Macarena Moves: The 6's

6   Hold right arm straight out in front of you with palm down.

12   Hold left arm out straight in front of you with palm down.

18   Turn right hand up.

24   Turn left palm up.

30   Right hand grabs upper left arm.

36   Left hand grabs upper right arm. (This forms an X across the chest.)

42	Place right hand behind neck and hold there.
48	Place left hand behind neck.
54	Place right hand on left front pocket and hold it there.
60	Place left hand on right front pocket and hold it there.
66	Place right hand on right back pocket.
72	Place left hand on left back pocket.

Refrain

Place hands on hips and move hips left.

Saying "Oh, the 6's!"

Move hips right. Move hips left.

Clap and jump 90 degrees to the right.

Repeat!

Repeat the refrain after each set.

4. Continue assigning a number to each of the other macarena motions as you work through the set. If there are more motions than multiples, return to the start of the number set.

5. When you have modeled how the activity works and the class seems to understand it, ask a student to lead. Start with an easy set of facts, like the one's, two's, and five's. The participants will catch on to the beat, the motions, and the procedure. Then tackle more challenging number sets.

Variation: Have a "yell time" for a drill exercise outside and a "whisper time" for inside drills to the macarena beat.

Activity: Continents in My World (Social Studies)

Students act out placement of the continents on a world map in this activity. Everyone faces a large world map or an imaginary map.

1. Spread arms out to the side with palms facing out, as if you were about to give someone a big hug. Bring your right arm across in front of you and touch your left hand with your right hand as you say, "North America."

2. Point to your forehead with both hands as you say, "Europe."

3. Hold arms out as before. Bring left hand across the front of you and touch the right hand as you say, "Asia."

4. Place hands on waist. Move hips in a circle. Say, "Equator." Move one hand a few inches above the waist and one hand a few inches below the waist as you say, "Africa is on the equator."

5. Touch the left knee as you say, "South America is under North America."

6. Touch the right knee as you say, "Australia is under Asia."

7. Touch the floor as you say, "Antarctica."

Variation: Make the moves to a song.

Sing the Continents

(Adapt to the tune of "Are You Sleeping?")

First comes North America.
Europe, Asia
Africa's at the equator
South America's under North America.
Australia's under Asia
Antarctica's way down below.
Those are our continents.

OTHER MEMORY TRIGGERS

Just as actors continually learn new acting techniques, students continually add memory-control devices to their repertoire of memory skills as they become more experienced in test taking.

Chunking

Chunking refers to the strategy of breaking a large information set into smaller bits. The amount of information a learner can hold in memory depends on the individual's memory capacity. Play memory games with students to identify how many words or numbers they can recall. When presenting large amounts of information or skills, divide it into chunks or groups that match the student's ability to remember it. Gradually increase the size of the information chunks to expand the student's memory skills and capacity. Use this technique with vocabulary lists, words in a series, steps, or procedures. Show students how to break down long data sets they encounter into workable chunks.

Categorizing

An effective strategy for remembering items is to categorize them. This is a way of finding a home for the information to be used, understood, and stored. Remembering these items is easy because they are mentally placed under a heading. It is easier to memorize a list of animals, if you break the list into subcategories such as mammals, farm animals, and jungle animals. Students learning Spanish vocabulary might categorize items into words that are like English (*famosa—famous*), unlike English (*casa—house*), and "false friends" (*nombre—name*, not *number*). We start teaching young children at early ages classifying, sorting, and categorizing. Continue to practice these useful skills at all ages and levels. Create categories from students' interests and hobbies for timed practice.

Activity: Applying Chunking and Categorizing to Spelling

Often spelling lists are assigned, and a weekly spelling test is administered. Then the class quickly forgets the words. Bring more meaning into spelling exercises by following these steps.

1. Divide the words into groups of seven. Introduce them in "chunks."

2. Use the targeted words within your units of study. Ask students to categorize them and to make other associations. Model strategies to categorize words into groups.

Pegging

Peg words are used as a place to "hang" other words. Pegging is a fun way of remembering dry facts. The information can be pegged or connected in a familiar sequence, story, visual, rhyme, jingle, chant, or saying.

Activity: Peg Link or Chain

Connect one name or word to the next through imaginary visual connections. Outrageous connections are often easier to remember. For example, in order to remember the names of the first five United States astronauts—Alan Shepard, J. Walter Schirra, Virgil Grissom, John Glenn, and Scott Carpenter—try this. Picture a shepherd (Shepard) shearing (Shirra) his sheep facing a grizzly (Grissom) bear in the glen (Glenn) but he is rescued by a carpenter (Carpenter). In this case, a set of names are pegged to mental images in a chain. Challenge your class to create a peg chain for information they need to learn, such as the names of the early presidents or the countries of South America.

Mind Joggers

Students can add the following mind joggers to their repertoire of memory-control strategies.

- Make a time line. Students plot data on a sequential line with each significant event located at a certain point in time.
- Create tables and charts. Students organize new information in graphic form. For example, students can chart units of measurement during a metric study. They can then refer to the chart until the knowledge is transferred to their memory banks. Students often picture a chart in their minds to retrieve the information for tests.
- Sketch the problem. Students draw their own pictures of a concept or information set. This transfers information from a written source to an image on paper to an image in the mind.

PRACTICE, PRACTICE, PRACTICE

The best way to learn juggling, tossing a Frisbee, cooking, painting, or any skill, is to practice. Michael Jordan is considered the greatest basketball player of the twentieth century, but he had to practice regularly. Students know they need to exercise if they want to keep their muscles in shape. The same is true for the mind. To get the top performance from memory, they need to exercise it. Suggest to students that, when they are bored or have extra time, they can improve their minds by memorizing lists, dates, or facts. They should practice the information until it becomes nearly effortless to recall, like walking.

Unfortunately, young people don't always realize how much they will need the skills and information they learn in school when they reach adulthood. Students will want to know their math facts in order to perform daily tasks easily and automatically, without the assistance of a calculator or manipulatives. To inspire practice, show students that improving memory skills is both fun and necessary.

Memory Cues

The following techniques provide a memory workout. Individuals who practice them hone their ability to recall information and images.

Activity: Observation (Teacher Dialogue)

Police officers and detectives develop strong observation skills to recall details. You can increase your observation skills anytime, in public, without saying a word or disturbing anyone. When you are waiting in a line or in a crowd, observe the people around you (without staring, of course). Look at an individual carefully and then look away. Recall as many details about the person as you can. Regular practice of this technique greatly increases your memory capacity. Who knows? You may be a valuable witness to a major robbery some day.

Variation: Use a photograph of a group of people.

1. Study a group picture of classmates, movie stars, or strangers in the newspaper.

2. Visualize the individuals in the group.

3. Look away and see how many people you can describe or recall.

4. Tell a friend.

Activity: Remembering Lists

1. Make a list of things in a specific category, such as a row of numbers, a set of attributes, or a list of proper names.
    Lists for memory practice:

    -   The fifty states
    -   The state capitals
    -   Oceans of the world
    -   Standard and metric measurements
    -   Poems
    -   Names, faces, and positions of school support staff
    -   Super Bowl winners
    -   Famous men or women in sports
    -   Major bodies in the solar system

2. Study the list, then hide it.

3. See how many items you can remember!

METAMEMORY: STUDENTS TAKE CENTER STAGE

Metamemory is adapted from the term metacognition, which refers to the practice of analyzing your own thinking processes. Metamemory, therefore, is looking into memory and knowing how you remember information. Students need to know memory skills and strategies, but they also need to be aware that they can control what they remember.

Before, during, and after memory activities in your class, ask students to reflect on the workings of their own memories. What strategies work best for each student? What kinds of information present the most challenge? Self-reflection is itself an excellent memory tool; facts, information, and concepts are retained when self-talk is used. More than that, however, reflection allows students to become more self-directed learners.

Memory plays a major role in each actor's success. A character's lines, actions, and emotions must be recalled and performed on cue. Infuse memory tips, tricks, and hooks in all subject areas to help students internalize techniques for storing information and ideas in long-term memory. Students can then retrieve the facts and skills for major performances on tests and in life.

As directors/teachers, one of the greatest gifts we can give learners is independence. Eventually, we have to step off the stage and let the student perform. The strategies and activities in this chapter will help students assume control of the process of building strong long-term memories. Eventually, they become directors themselves, by learning to set the scene with the right props and cues to help them rebuild the memory when they need it.

We close this chapter on memory with lyrics from a song, because, as we have said, songs are memory tools that convey ideas. The purpose of this song is to remind educators to teach the curriculum in a variety of exciting, stimulating ways that challenge minds to produce thinkers and problem solvers.

Brighten Up My Every Day

(from Carolyn Chapman's *Making the Shoe Fit*, song by Connie Ryals)

(Refrain)

Sing it, dance it, paint it, shake it
Think it, play it, draw it, bake it.
Brighten up my every day
With awesome ways that I can learn.

Don't just give me paper . . . pencil
'Cause I need much more you know.
All that is expected of me
And all I will need to learn and grow.

(Repeat refrain)

Don't just tell me how to do it
But help me think from day to day
I might just surprise and fool you
When I get the answer my own way.

(Repeat refrain)

I know there's a time to just sit and learn from you
And paper and pencil are also learning tools
But much of the time I need to challenge my mind
So brighten up my every day with all these ways.

(Repeat refrain)

Preparing the 5
Performer

Internal Readiness for Tests

The Test-Ready Performer

Brain: Relaxed and alert; ready to release stored information

Body: Relaxed and dressed for the test

Ears: Ready to listen attentively

Hands: Ready to transfer information from my brain to the test

Heart: Filled with desire to do my best

SELF-REGULATED LEARNING

Students need to know that they control what they learn. Internal control, or self-regulated learning, determines their success on tests as well as their accomplishments in other aspects of their lives. The ultimate goal of teaching test-taking skills is to transfer their knowledge to the test format so they perform well as responsible, expert learners. This chapter is filled with ideas, tips, and activities to teach students how to identify and control their own thinking and become test ready. Test-ready students prepare their brains, bodies, and minds for test day. They develop positive and appropriate habits and skills to employ during the test. After tests, they reflect on their own performance. Finally, all year they work to develop habits and attitudes that see them through to success. As the director of this production, teach students internal control methods to use before, during, and after the test. Remember to foster test success skills and positive attitudes toward assessments all year.

BEFORE THE TEST: BRAIN READINESS

Performers of all types, including actors on the stage and athletes on the playing field, strive to be physically prepared. Actors avoid voice strain and keep their bodies in shape. Runners stretch and avoid activities, such as smoking, that might damage the healthy lungs that give them speed. For testing, the most important physical instrument student-performers use is the brain. The brain is the control center for learning; it is the place where memory and thinking are processed. Students need to understand basic brain functions and various ways to keep the brain in top condition for high achievement and test success.

Introducing Students to the Brain, the Control Center for Learning

There are many ways to teach students about the brain. Use or adapt the following approaches to convey this important information.

Activity: Brain Control—Teacher Script

The following script develops understanding of how the brain works.

You have the most intricate and delicate control center ever known. It has marvelous abilities. Your personal control center, your brain, is with you at all times. You take your control center everywhere you go. It works for you 24/7. It even works for you while you are sleeping.

How much does this phenomenal control center cost? (Wait for response.) Each of you has one of these control centers. It does not cost anything, but its value cannot be measured.

How is your brain protected from damage? (Wait for response.) Feel the strong, protective skull that covers your brain. It is there because your brain cannot be replaced.

What part does your brain play in what you learn? (Wait for response.)

This miraculous brain controls everything you learn. Remember, YOU control what your brain learns and what it can do.

Activity: Wiggle Control

1. Tell students, "Your brain will work for you with just a silent command. Wiggle your little finger."

2. Ask students, "Who made your finger move?" Explain, "You told your brain to wiggle it, and then your brain sent messages through your body to your finger."

3. Tell students to point to the person who is in charge of this great control center. When students point to themselves, use the following statement as a lead-in to a discussion: "Yes, you are the one responsible for everything you learn and do."

Activity: The Brain at Work

Name the many, many ways your brain is working and learning at this moment. Complete this sentence: My brain is controlling my _____. The answers may include breathing, blood flow, vision, digestion, senses, emotions, movements, thinking, and memory.

Variations:
- Invent a brain song with the refrain, "My brain is controlling my. . . ." Response examples include memory, thinking, focus, movements, and attitude.
- Draw a picture titled "My Brain at Work."

Brain Facts

The brain has long been a mystery, but neurologists, the specialists who study the nervous system, now use modern technology to examine how the brain works. New discoveries are made every day. Consider sharing with students some of this fascinating information, particularly how it relates to test success. Introducing one brain fact or brain structure each day over the course of a few weeks can be fun and very useful. To get you started, Figure 5.1 provides information about brain function highlights for test success.

However brain knowledge is conveyed, it guides learners to place test preparation activities into a context. Let students know they can train their brains to work better and harder for test success.

FIGURE 5.1

Brain Function Highlights for Test Success

Description	Role in Test Success
Cerebrum The cerebrum is the largest part of the brain. It is divided into two halves called the right and left hemisphere.	Thinking, perceiving, and moving are among the jobs of the cerebrum. The cerebrum processes everything you learn throughout life, including material for tests. Memories to help answer questions are filed in this section of the learning brain.
Cerebral Cortex The cortex is composed of six layers of gray cells that cover the cerebrum like the bark on a tree. If the cortex could be laid out flat, it would be about the size of a large sheet of construction paper, six layers deep.	The cortex participates in perception, attention, planning, decision making, and memory. These skills are crucial for learning and test taking.
Corpus Callosum The corpus callosum connects the hemispheres of the global and critical thinking cerebrum. These nerve fibers let the hemispheres communicate with each other.	Connections between hemispheres allow for creative, global, and critical thinking. The brain becomes more prepared for tests through experiences that engage the left and right hemispheres.
Subcortical Area The subcortical brain structures, also known as limbic areas, help to regulate information related to survival and identity. Specifically, the almond-shaped amygdala plays a key role in activating fear reactions. A subcortical pathway conveys information about potential threats to the amygdala, which produces positive or negative responses.	Sweating, heart pounding, and rapid breathing are a few symptoms of text anxiety. Often these reactions create an emergency response pattern called the fight or flight response. These reactions can interfere with a student's ability to stay calm and focus. Successful test-takers know how to recognize and control their "gut" responses. A positive testing environment supports optimal brain functioning.
Nervous System The nervous system (the brain, spinal cord, nerves, and sensory receptors) processes information from outside and inside the body. This system is the "Internet" or "phone system" of the body, with the brain as the control center.	The nervous system, by design, takes in information from our surroundings so we can react. However, during a test, physical and emotional reactions to distractions in the environment may override the pathways or networks for thinking. Successful test takers learn to cope with distractions.

	Teachers and other adults should try to reduce distractions during tests. If the school staff and parents are highly stressed about the test, these feelings can easily be passed to students and affect their performances and attitudes.
Brain Cells (Neurons) A neuron is shaped like a hand and arm. Dendrites are fingerlike extensions on the cell's "palm" (cell body) that bring in information that is sent along the axon, or "arm." Neurons communicate by passing electrochemical impulses from one cell to another. The impulse, or message, starts in the dendrites, travels along the axon, and is released into the synapse, or space between nerve cells in the brain. The message then jumps across the synapse to the next nerve cell. Neurons are organized into memory networks.	Strong long-term memories are formed when information has emotional and personal importance to the learner and is likely to be needed again. As memories are consolidated, the brain reflects the changes. Connections between neurons strengthen. Learning forms new neural patterns throughout life. However, neural connections are fragile. Without ongoing reinforcement, they wither away. Numerous factors contribute to the formation of more, stronger connections between neurons and a brain that is especially ready to learn. The factors include a rich, challenging learning environments; personal and emotional links to information; and opportunities to work with information in a variety of contexts.

Note: Since our understanding of the brain changes almost daily, update and supplement this information as needed. Also, adapt the vocabulary and content to the grade level, interests, and needs of your students.

My Great Brain

(To the tune of "Mary Had a Little Lamb")
My great brain weighs three to five pounds,
Three to five pounds, three to five pounds.
My great brain weighs three to five pounds
And has 100 billion cells.

Each tiny cell has hairlike dendrites,
Hairlike dendrites, hairlike dendrites.
Each tiny cell has hairlike dendrites
That gather information.

Every single cell has one long axon,
One long axon, one long axon.

Every single cell has one long axon
To send out information.

The space between the cells is called a synapse,
Called a synapse, called a synapse.
The space between the cells is called a synapse.
It transports what I have learned.

Metaphors for Brain Functioning

Metaphors assist students in visualizing how the brain works. For example, ask students to consider how the brain is like the Internet. Discuss the value of making personal connections to information to assist the brain in processing information. The comparisons will be incomplete but are useful in developing the students' understanding of the brain using familiar terms.

Activity: Exploring Metaphors

- Have students create brain metaphors. Start with this prompt: A brain is like a _____ because they both _____.
- Try these comparisons: a computer, Pony Express, telephone lines, filing cabinets.

Activity: Egg Drop Contest

1. Have students create a container to hold an egg. The challenge is to design a package to keep the egg safe so it will not break when dropped from the height of a two-story building.

2. Complete the egg drop in a safe place.

3. Commend and reward students whose eggs did not crack.

4. Ask, "How is your skull like an eggshell?" Discuss how the skull protects the brain like an eggshell protects the egg.

5. Discuss ways to protect the brain. Examples: helmets, ear plugs, appropriate lighting and noise levels, healthy foods, and general safety precautions.

BEFORE THE TEST: BODY READINESS

Performers need to be in good physical condition to do their best. We've included information and a checklist to help students prepare their bodies for test day.

Eating for Top Performance

Good nutrition is essential for concentration and thinking ability. Use the charts shown in Figure 5.2, Feeding Your Brain, and Figure 5.3, The Brain Training Nutrition Checklist, with students and parents to emphasize the value of a quality diet for learning and test success. The brain's junk food is any food that interferes with thinking. Students need to recognize the foods to eat and foods to avoid before tests. Challenge everyone to add other foods to this list.

FIGURE 5.2	
Feeding Your Brain	
Foods That Increase Brain Power	*Foods That Decrease Brain Power*
Proteins • serve many functions, including carrying oxygen in blood, building muscles, and fighting infection. • are necessary for the function of neurotransmitters that are responsible for carrying information between brain cells and thus to stay alert, to listen, and to think quickly. ▶ **Key sources:** beef, fish, chicken, dried peas, beans, eggs, milk products	**Excess Sugar** • reduces the ability to concentrate and learn in some people. • depresses immunity, contributing to poor performance and missed days. ▶ **Key sources:** sweetened cereal, candy, cookies, soft drinks
Carbohydrates • provide physical and mental energy. • maintain mental energy without producing a sugar slump when derived from certain sources such as fruit, cereals, and grains, vegetables, and legumes. • help increase the brain's level of serotonin, which contributes to a sense of well-being. ▶ **Key sources:** bread, whole grains, vegetables, fruits	**Artificial Flavorings and Preservatives** *(MSG, FD&C Yellow Dye #5, Sulfites . . .)* • can cause allergic reactions in sensitive individuals. ▶ **Key sources:** fast foods, dried fruit, processed foods containing additives
Fats • provide energy. • assist in the absorption of fat-soluble vitamins. • build brain tissue (some fatty acids). • contribute to formation of insulating sheath around each nerve. ▶ **Key sources:** meat, fish, poultry, nuts, eggs, milk products	**Caffeine** • can cause the "jitters" and interfere with concentration. • may create a need for more frequent bathroom breaks. ▶ **Key sources:** chocolate, sodas, cocoa, coffee, tea

(Continued)

FIGURE 5.2 (Continued)

Vitamins

- are body helpers (13 vitamins essential to human life for many functions).
- assist in converting carbohydrates to produce energy and to assemble proteins.
- help body heal and build up immune system.
- are often lacking. Children's diets often are deficient in vitamin C, vitamin A, folic acid, and vitamin B_6.

▶ **Key sources:** fruits, vegetables, grains

Minerals (*calcium, iron, zinc, magnesium . . .*)

- are important to nervous system functioning.
- help form bone and blood (calcium for bone and iron for blood).
- are often lacking. Children's diets are often deficient in calcium and iron.

▶ **Key sources:** nuts, eggs, milk products, dried fruits, whole grains, some vegetables, organ meats

Excess Processed (Hydrogenated) Fat

- Can interfere with brain function.

▶ **Key sources:** processed cookies, crackers, bakery products, deep-fried foods, margarine

---

FIGURE 5.3

Brain Training Nutrition Checklist

Check the items that describe your nutrition habits:

- ☐ Eat regular meals.
- ☐ Eat foods rich in iron, vitamin C, zinc, calcium, and vitamin E.
- ☐ Drink plenty of water.
- ☐ Eat foods containing complex carbohydrates.
- ☐ Keep the amount of fat in your diet reasonable.
- ☐ Eat fruits and vegetables.
- ☐ Omit caffeine products.

Set goals. Write the key changes you want to make to better feed your brain.

Physical Exercise

Physical exercise enhances thinking by releasing endorphins. Endorphins produce a calming effect on the nervous system and enhance thinking. Physical exercise provides more oxygen to the brain. It rejuvenates alertness and thinking. For these reasons, physical education classes and recess should be held on test days. Remember, when a student is seated too long, the brain loses its edge, so intersperse physical activity before and between test segments.

BEFORE THE TEST: MENTAL READINESS

Learners need to condition their minds as well as their bodies for tests. As a director of the testing scene, prepare your performers mentally for the roles they have on test day. Performers do best when they have a feeling of control and when people around them have positive attitudes. The following activities, exercises, and tips will help you and your students achieve mental readiness for tests.

Removing Unknowns: A Key to Brain Control

In most instances, students have no idea why standardized tests are given or how the scores will be used. The vocabulary of testing is unfamiliar to them. These unknowns skew results, because many learners know the tested information but do not know the strategies to apply what they know to the terminology of the test format. It is not fair to give a standardized test to students with many unknowns. In doing so, it is like asking them to perform a role without telling them about the play. Just as we would not expect student drivers to pass their exams without practicing turns or parking, we should not expect top performance from students who have not practiced test-taking strategies. The unknowns also elevate anxiety levels. Discussions, explanations, and practice tests alleviate these feelings.

The first step in erasing test unknowns is to introduce students to the test's purpose and how it will be used. The following script may be adapted and used to introduce standardized testing.

Getting to Know the Standardized Test: Teacher Script

Students in schools across our country took a test like the one you are going to take. They followed the same rules during the test that you will be given. Their combined and averaged scores set a norm, or score, that you are expected to make. When we receive your scores, we will know if you scored above or below this typical norm.

After all students finish, the answer sheets go to a central place where they are graded and scored by a machine. The machine reads all the little bubbles you filled in to tell if the answers are right or wrong. Our class will receive a score, and that score will be combined with the scores of other boys and girls in our school who are in the same grade level. The scores for each grade will also be compared to the scores of students in the same grade level in other schools.

The most important thing to remember is that your teachers will look at your score to see what you need to learn to improve. They will know to work on certain areas to improve the total class score. Also, the principal and other school leaders will look at the results to see if our school has improved since last year. The newspaper will publish the overall score of each school in our area for everyone to see.

Your work on this test will not make you pass or fail, but remember that teachers and parents will look at your scores to see how much you have learned this year. Don't forget, it is very important to "show what you know." Always do your very best on each section so we will know how much you learned and how to help you.

Introducing Standardized Test Terms

Be aware of using terms related to standardized tests that students may not understand. Define or explain testing vocabulary in simple terms so the learners feel more comfortable with it. The Standardized Testing Vocabulary chart in Figure 5.4 can be adapted and used with students and parents.

Activity: Testing, Testing, One, Two, Three

Individually, in pairs, or as a class, ask students to brainstorm reasons they need to know how to take tests. Create a list of the responses. Lead a discussion session of the results. Before the session ends, you may want to share the list that follows:

- To show what you know to teachers, parents, and yourself
- To pass your classes. In every subject, every year you will take chapter tests, unit tests, midsemester tests, achievement tests, and final or exit exams
- To obtain a driver's license
- To win competitive thinking games
- To enter and succeed in college

FIGURE 5.4

Standardized Testing Vocabulary

Standardized Testing Vocabulary	For the Teacher	For the Students
Criterion-Referenced Test	A criterion-referenced test measures how well students mastered specific content, standards, or skills. Since these tests show how much targeted material students mastered, the results can be used to plan instruction, to evaluate progress, and to improve teaching.	This test shows us what you have learned. We will be able to see what you know and what you don't know, so we can help you.
Norm-Referenced Test	A norm-referenced test measures how well students perform compared to other students of the same grade who took the same test. All scores are compared against a norm, or the "typical" performance the test makers have seen in sample tests. Half of the students in the norm group scored above the norm, and half scored below it.	The test will let us know if you scored higher or lower than other students who took the test.
Percentile	Percentile scores range from 1 to 99. They do not represent the percentage of questions the student answered correctly but rather the percentage of students who received lower scores. For example, a student in the 95th percentile performed better than 95 percent of other students who took the test.	The percentile tells us if your score is at the bottom, middle, or top of the scores earned by other students who took the test.
Raw Score	The raw score equals the number of questions answered correctly.	The raw score tells us how many of your answers were correct.
Standardized Test	Standardized tests have specific, fixed, and uniform formats and guidelines for administration of the test. They are scored in a uniform way, usually by a machine. The results are usually compared to a norm, or median performance of students in a test group who took the test.	When a test is standardized, it is given in the same way; within the same time limits; using identical rules, directions, and materials. The scores are compared to how other students at your level performed on the test.

- To take a test for a job
- To win a large sum of money on a game show
- To make your dreams come true!

BEFORE THE TEST: IDENTIFYING AND CONTROLLING TEST ANXIETY

All performers experience anxiety at some point. Students may be nervous before the test because they are worried about passing to the next grade level, having bad grades, bubbling in, or completing the test within time limits. Fears such as these easily become barriers to thinking.

Physical Reactions to Test Stress

Headaches	Anger
Nausea	Fidgeting
Sleepiness	Inappropriate laughter
Poor bladder control	Emotional outbursts
Perspiration	

Bad Stress and Good Stress

Bad Stress

Bad stress is the negative feeling that occurs when you want to get away from an event or situation. Stress can be caused by the thought of anything that makes you uncomfortable. Fear is a stress that is felt when there is a real threat. Anxiety is a feeling you have when you think there is something to dread or fear.

The nervous system responds to the fear of tests in the same way it responds to the fear of an approaching wild animal. When tests cause excessive nervousness or tension, students' autonomic nervous systems react and send signals that physically prepare the individual to deal with the situation. The nervous system goes into an emergency response mode, notifies the body to produce adrenaline, and prepares to protect itself through fight-or-flight defense patterns. Thinking and creativity can be blocked because the mind is busy making plans for a physical reaction to the threat (Howard, 2000).

"Before tests I feel nervous. I get butterflies!"

Parker Bell, sixth grader

Good Stress

Good stress occurs when adrenaline produces a surge of energy accompanied by anticipation and the excitement of a challenge. This "psyched up" feeling enhances performance. Students need to know that "butterflies in the stomach" and "the jitters" may indicate healthy levels of concern for test success. Remind them that some of the greatest actors experience stage fright. The validation that it is okay to be nervous will have a calming effect on the students.

Diagnosing and Treating Test Anxiety

As the testing director, you need to identify and eliminate sources of anxiety or bad stress caused by tests to enhance concentration. A perceptive teacher sees, hears, and recognizes signs of anxiety in students before tests are given. For example, anxiety may be seen in a student's eyes that appear large with apprehension. Tight muscles and nervous jitters are obvious, too. Address these negative reactions when the first signs of anxiety are observed, prior to the first test being given at the beginning of the year.

Over time, your observations will reveal whether the student's anxiety manifests itself as a trait or a state. In other words, the anxiety may be one of the individual's personal characteristics, or it may be a temporary reaction to performing and being evaluated. It is also possible that the anxiety is related to the tested subject; some students become nervous during tests in particular content areas. Confidence may fluctuate based on the material covered. Also, look to yourself and other adults as potential sources of anxiety. A parent, teacher, or administrator who exhibits high levels of test anxiety easily transfers the feelings to students and hinders their performance.

One obvious cause of anxiety is the fear of failure. Assure students that their test scores will not be used to make a pass or fail decision. They need to know they will not be punished for low scores. Work with individual students to identify test concerns and their causes (see Figure 5.5). Then provide strategies for approaching problems to overcome fear and present tasks as challenges. In this section, we include a variety of tools to help your students understand and overcome test anxiety. Use Figure 5.6, Assessing Assessment Anxiety, and Figure 5.7, Getting Yourself Ready, to gain understanding of a student's anxiety.

FIGURE 5.5

How to Overcome Fears	
Specific Fear	How to Overcome It
• I will forget information. • I may not complete the test. • I won't live up to expectations. • I can't do it! (low confidence). • The test will ask stuff I don't know. • I feel like giving up.	• Use memory hooks. • Practice pacing. • Know the terminology and listen; always do your best. • Know test strategies. • Know you can do it; use positive self-talk. • Answer easy questions first. • Learn perseverance.

Use the relaxation exercises below to teach anxiety control.

Exercises to Reduce Anxiety

Students can take control of their own performance by developing a repertoire of exercises specifically designed to reduce anxiety. We include a few examples.

Relaxation Exercise: From the Deep

1. Close your eyes and sit in a comfortable position.

2. Breathe from deep within your abdomen.

3. Place your hand on your abdomen. Feel your breath there.

4. Count to four as you take a long, deep breath, filling your lungs with air. Feel your abdomen expand.

5. Hold this breath for a count of two.

6. Exhale slowly for a count of four.

7. Rest for a count of two.

8. Count to four as you take a long, deep breath, filling your lungs.

9. Hold this breath for a count of four.

10. Exhale slowly to a count of four.

11 Rest for a count of two.

12. Repeat this exercise for five minutes.

13. During each repetition, concentrate on relaxing a part of the body. Try relaxing the face, jaws, neck, back, and stomach.

FIGURE 5.6

Assessing Assessment Anxiety

	Always	Often	Sometimes	Rarely
1. I feel good about taking tests.	4	3	2	1
2. I worry when tests are mentioned.	4	3	2	1
3. I always score high on tests.	4	3	2	1
4. I am nervous before tests.	4	3	2	1
5. It is easy for me to recall information.	4	3	2	1
6. I feel sick before tests.	4	3	2	1
7. I know how to control my thinking.	4	3	2	1
8. I have trouble keeping my mind on the test.	4	3	2	1
9. I know how to prepare myself for tests.	4	3	2	1
10. I get flustered and run out of time during tests.	4	3	2	1

Note: If you answered with high numbers (threes and fours) on odd-numbered items, then your test anxiety is probably low. If you answered with high numbers (threes and fours) on even-numbered items, then your test anxiety level is probably high. Your teacher can help by giving you anxiety control strategies.

FIGURE 5.7

Getting Yourself Ready: A Checklist

When preparing for a test, how often do you . . .

	Frequently	Sometimes	Never
1. Know test-taking skills?			
2. Know how to apply test-taking strategies?			
3. Know the content?			
4. Use relaxation exercises?			
5. Prepare yourself physically?			
6. Prepare yourself emotionally?			
7. Ask yourself, "What is the worst thing that will happen if my score is low?"			
8. Organize the supplies and materials you need?			
9. Know strategies to jog your memory?			
10. Think of the test as a puzzle or challenging game?			
11. Think of ways you learn best?			
12. Plan a personal reward or celebration after a test?			
13. Remind yourself that you are smart?			

Relaxation Exercise: Robot/Rag Doll Walk

The following exercises demonstrate how breathing changes during tense and relaxed states.

1. Robot Walk. Stiffen and tense the body while walking. Your breathing will be shallow.

2. Rag Doll Walk. Walk with a limber, relaxed body. Your breathing will become relaxed and deep.

3. Have students compare their feelings after completing the Robot Walk and the Rag Doll Walk.

BEFORE THE TEST: BUILDING CONFIDENCE

Confidence is a direct reflection of past experiences. It is the trust students have in their own abilities. This self-trust is a major component of positive attitudes toward testing. Students who lack self-confidence may display various behaviors. They often cheat because they want to have good scores and do not want to disappoint the teachers, parents, and other important people in their lives. Other students may appear to have an "I don't care" attitude, a cover-up for low self-confidence. Confidence is a major key to approaching a test in a relaxed, controlled, savvy way.

Confidence Indicator Checklist

High	Low
☐ Raises hand often	☐ Seldom raises hand
☐ Concentrates	☐ Is easily distracted
☐ Focuses eyes on the teacher	☐ Avoids eye contact with the teacher
☐ Is independent	☐ Depends on notes, peers, teacher

Talking Your Way to Success

No doubt you have experienced a difficult moment in school, work, sports, or personal relationships in which you used self-talk to keep up your confidence. Or, you may have talked yourself into failing. The same is true for students. They need to learn to employ appropriate, positive phrases.

Turning Negative Self-Talk Into Positive

Students approach a test with negative messages on their minds and lips for a variety of reasons. Perhaps they are taking the test in a negative environment, have had bad experiences in the past, or simply are going through a bout of natural performance anxiety. Whatever the causes, the following statements are examples of negative self-talk:

- "My parents will be so upset if I don't do well on this test!"
- "I hate tests!"
- "I just want to get this over with!"
- "I will fail if my score is not high."
- "I feel sick."
- "I won't be able to go to college if I don't do well on this test."

Teachers unintentionally induce stress with comments similar to the following:

- "We won't have recess or do anything fun during test week."
- "This test will be hard for you, so . . ."
- "Our principal will be upset if our school doesn't have high scores."
- "I don't want to do this any more than you do."

These comments may instill fear of failure and cause performance anxiety, especially when a student's "need to please" is immense. Students often parrot and learn to believe in the messages they hear from adults. It is especially important that you, as the testing director, convey positive messages about testing.

Positive teacher messages include the following:

- "We will celebrate our hard work when the test is completed."
- "We have a chance to show how much we learned."
- "Our principal wants you to do your best."
- "We will work together. We have a great team."
- "Use the test tools we practiced all year."

Confidence Builders

Not only do you need to be sure that your message is positive, you also need to teach students to use positive self-talk. Use Figure 5.8: Confidence Builders Checklist with students. These affirmations are designed to create feelings of success.

Dress for Test Success

When class members perceive themselves as looking and feeling good on test days, they have more self-confidence. For instance, if a student wears a favorite or lucky shirt, pleasant feelings are connected with test experiences. The class may design a T-shirt or thinking cap with a logo to wear on test days. Logo samples include "Dressed for the Test," "Brain Trained for Testing," and "My Brain's Best on the Test!"

Other dress-for-success dos and don'ts are summarized below. Clothing and accessories should not distract but make the wearer feel positive and comfortable on test days.

Dress for Success

Dos	Don'ts
• Wear your favorite T-shirt.	• Wear uncomfortable clothes.
• Wear comfortable clothes.	• Use strong cologne or perfume.
• Wear favorite colors.	• Wear shoes with lights or bells.
• Wear a test-taking T-shirt.	• Wear shirts with extra-long sleeves.
• Wear quiet accessories.	• Wear shirts with thick or heavy cuffs.
	• Wear jewelry that jingles.

FIGURE 5.8

Confidence Builders Checklist

Directions: Select five confidence builders from the list below. Place check marks by your choices. Before a test, repeat your chosen confidence builders silently to yourself.

☐ I have the support and encouragement I need.

☐ Learning and remembering are easy for me.

☐ My memory is alert.

☐ My mind is in high gear.

☐ I'm confident. I can do this!

☐ My mind is working effectively and efficiently.

☐ I remember what I need to do to succeed.

☐ I'm optimistic!

☐ I listen carefully.

☐ My mind is open.

☐ Look what I can do!

☐ I'm ready!

☐ I love this stuff.

☐ I'm achieving my goals.

☐ _____

Student and Teacher Comfort: A Summary

You and your students build confidence by preparing carefully for test day. The more comfortable you are, the better you will perform when the curtain goes up. Here is a summary of conditions for the comfort of both student performers and the testing director on test day. You may want to share the Conditions for Testing Comfort chart in Figure 5.9 with teachers, administrators, and students.

FIGURE 5.9

Conditions for Testing Comfort

Discomfort	Comfort
Student	Student
• doesn't know what to expect. • can't apply the information. • has many tardies or absences. • doesn't feel sense of belonging or part of the group. • doesn't feel self-confident. • has the feeling of being controlled. • has a fear of failure. • feels pressured to perform. • is expected to act or try like someone else.	• feels there are no or few unknowns. • knows the material. • feels bonded or team atmosphere. • has an at-home feeling. • feels in control. • is self-confident. • possesses internal desire to do the best job. • is accepted for self. • has a team spirit for success. • is familiar with the test administrator and proctor.
Teacher	Teacher
• is late getting materials and thoughts organized. • feels others have unrealistic expectations. • is confused by directions and guidelines. • wears uncomfortable clothes. • is anxious over test-taking behaviors. • waited too long to start preparing students with test-taking skills. • knows students haven't mastered all test-related areas.	• is prepared. • understands procedures. • has administrative support. • dresses appropriately. • has confidence in students. • has prepared students thoroughly. • has a test-ready mind-set.

DURING THE TEST: DEALING WITH DISTRACTIONS

Distractions are interruptions that take the mind away from the current task. They are aspects of the physical environment that interfere with academic performance, such as odd noises, smells, or lights that are very bright or dim. Some distractions come from other people, who may cough, shuffle, or whistle. Luckily, many of these factors can be controlled. Teach students how to cope with distractions.

Types of Distractions

Not all individuals are distracted by the same things. For example, some people are more productive when music plays while they work. They find that it helps them concentrate. Others need silence while they work. It is difficult for educators to satisfy the personal needs of all students all the time. However, awareness of various types of common distractions can prevent and solve many problems on test day. The Common Types of Distractions chart in Figure 5.10 summarizes the most typical ones.

FIGURE 5.10	
Common Types of Distractions	
Internal	sleepiness or tiredness from lack of sleep; hunger or thirst; stress or anxiety; restlessness or boredom; illness and its symptoms; outside thoughts, such as thoughts about problems at home
Visual	light and movement from computer screens; colors, walls, scenes outside; posters, banners, and pictures; movement of test administrators and proctors
Auditory	bells; other people talking; motors on heating and cooling units; outside traffic noises; coughing, sneezing, or shuffling; buzz of lights or computers; telephone ringing; new, strange, or different voice administering the test

Tuning Out Distractions

The best way to learn concentration is to practice. During practice tests and rehearsals, challenge students to concentrate despite your intentional distractions. Turn it into a game to see how well students ignore your bell ringing or loud coughing. Discuss "what if" scenarios like those shown in Figure 5.11. What if you hear a loud motor outside? What if you need a tissue?

Although the school's personnel can minimize distractions, some are inevitable. Students need to learn how to concentrate. Infuse these skills in routine test-taking experiences. Challenge learners to identify their distractions.

FIGURE 5.11	
Actions for Distractions	
What if . . .	What will you do?

1. someone talks?

2. another student is moving around?

3. there is a knock on the door?

4. you hear a siren?

5. there is a noise in the hallway?

6. someone coughs or sneezes?

7. your pencil lead breaks?

8. you need scratch paper?

9. you can't concentrate?

10. you need to go to the restroom?

11. you need a drink?

12. you lose your place?

13. you have a question about directions?

14. you don't feel well?

Desk Exercises

If students have trouble focusing because of anxiety, stress, or external distractions, they need ways to focus their bodies and minds on test performance. The following desk exercises may be used during tests because they are quiet, unobtrusive movements. Model and practice each exercise throughout the year in all subjects, in formal and informal testing situations. These exercises may be used in class, during tests, or in other situations at any time without disturbing people nearby, if used appropriately. Remind students not to disturb classmates with their actions.

Desk Exercise: Head and Neck

- Do a "turtle" movement as if moving the head in and out of shell.
- Nod slowly up and down.
- Tighten and relax neck muscles.

- Turn the head slowly from far left to far right.
- Bring the left ear to the left shoulder.
- Bring the right ear to the right shoulder.

Desk Exercise: Eyes

Tell students to keep the head still in the following exercise.

- Roll your eyes in a circle.
- Look far left and far right quickly.
- Look up and down quickly.
- Stare at a distant object.
- Open eyes as wide as possible.
- Squint.
- Blink repeatedly.

Desk Exercise: Hands, Arms, and Shoulders

- Stretch and tighten fingers individually and relax them.
- Make a tight fist. Stretch the fingers and relax the whole hand.
- Pretend to squeeze a soft rubber ball.
- Bend the wrist and move the hand in circles.
- Flex, tense, and relax the arm.
- Roll shoulders up, around, back, and forward.

Desk Exercise: Feet and Legs

- Use the "accelerator-pump," moving each foot up and down.
- Move each foot in a circle at the ankle.
- Move feet from side to side, like windshield wipers. Keep heels together.
- Straighten and bend each leg.
- Tighten and relax leg muscles.

Desk Exercise: Total Body

- Change from a relaxed posture to a rigid posture.
- Imagine the feeling of a line being drawn very slowly around your body.
- Tighten and relax individual muscles.

Desk Exercise: Focus the Mind

- Count backward, exhaling slowly.
- Take deep breaths and exhale each breath slowly.

- Play a quick mind game.
- Imagine being in your favorite vacation spot.
- Visualize a person you love or admire. Concentrate on that person.

DURING THE TEST: ESTABLISHING RESPECT FOR DIFFERENT TEST-TAKING STYLES

Each student has an individual test-taking style. These differences include reading rates, pacing, concentration, and thoroughness. For example, many students are embarrassed and intimidated when classmates complete a test while they are still working. Consider reading a version of the fable *The Tortoise and the Hare* to introduce a discussion of individual work pace.

Activity: Understanding Others' Needs

Explore and post ways to show respect for others to create a successful testing experience. The list may include the following:

- Show respect for everyone.
- Take turns. Raise your hand to ask a question.
- Listen when others ask questions.
- Remain quiet and still when you complete a test.

AFTER THE TEST: LEARNING TO COPE WITH FAILURE AND TAKE RISKS

Although mistakes and failures are a major part of learning, most individuals are easily embarrassed and ashamed by failure. Students need to understand the value of learning from failures and mistakes because these experiences teach some of life's greatest lessons. Share stories with students about famous people who experienced failure before succeeding. Discuss the fact that some of the biggest Broadway productions and many, many very successful actors and actresses experienced failure. Emphasize that failure is a valuable learning tool when it is used constructively.

Reasons for Test Failure

The causes of test failure are many. Some are listed in the chart below. After a student experiences failure on a test, work together to analyze the causes and develop a plan to improve.

Causes of Failure	Sources
Distractions	lack of sleep; hunger, physical discomfort, random thoughts, sustained periods of quiet, noise
Preparation	inadequate study skills/low attendance, lack of attention, unfamiliarity with test-taking strategies, poor memory skills
Internal Readiness	nervousness, memory blocks, negative self-talk (before, during, after), learned helpless ness, fear of failure, panic, lack of persistence
Confusion or Unfamiliarity	test format, layout, graphic designs, subject material, directions

Understanding the Value of Failure and Risks

Compare failure to goals missed in a basketball game. The goal is to get the ball in the basket to gain points, but in most games, there are more misses than hits. The challenge makes the players keep trying.

Activity: Missed Shots

1. Ask students to make a list of sports in which there are more misses than hits in the game.

2. Discuss the value of missed shots.

Activity: How Much Will I Risk?

Materials

- A goal created using a wastepaper basket
- A large paper wad or a soft sponge ball
- Masking tape, rope, or chalk

Procedure

1. Place a goal, such as a wastepaper basket, in a clear space in the classroom.

2. Use the tape, rope, or chalk to create three lines with each one a more challenging distance from the goal than the next. Explain that

the shot value from each line is as follows: 5 points for the line nearest the goal (lowest risk, lowest point value); 10 points for the middle line (medium risk, medium point value); 20 points from the line farthest from the goal (highest risk, highest point value).

3. Divide the class into two teams.

4. The student representing the team decides which goal line to use for tossing the ball into the goal. Remind students that there is more risk at the line farthest from the goal.

5. Post the score.

6. Call on individuals, alternating between teams. The first team to reach 100 points wins the game.

7. Lead a class discussion on the risk factors involved in the game and how it affected choices and decisions. For example, what makes a player choose a certain position? What risks are involved with each choice? Where do you take risks in other situations?

8. Ask students to compare the risks in the game to risks they take during a test.

Make-Up Tests Through a Student's Eyes

Some students consider missing a test a failure. They feel embarrassed and guilty when they have to complete a make-up test. They need to be taught otherwise. Students are usually absent for reasons out of their control, so the person administering make-up tests can convey the message that taking a make-up test is not a failure.

The make-up test may appear to be a punishment if the student has to miss a favorite subject or class time. If the test is administered while other students are attending a special event, a favorite class, or recess, the student may rush to complete the test or think more about the activities being missed than the items on the test. Give make-up tests under the best possible circumstances.

ALL YEAR: DEVELOPING TEST-TAKING SELF-AWARENESS

Successful test takers usually have a few qualities in common. They study all year, listen, seek and accept help when needed, and they understand the test directions. Most of all, they are self-aware learners. This self-knowledge, or test-taking self-awareness, is crucial for developing test success. If possible, bring veteran, successful student test takers into your classroom to share their expertise and allow your students to interview them. It will be heartening for them to hear how other students have done well on tests and to hear their accomplishments and advice.

Move students forward on this journey of self-knowledge all year. In this section, we include a variety of surveys, activities, and reflections you can use and adapt to guide students in developing test-taking self-awareness.

Ways of Learning

Students need to understand their own best ways of learning and their strongest forms of intelligence and how they impact test success. Learning style inventories and multiple intelligence tools are available. See Figure 5.12 for an informal questionnaire to use with your students.

I've Got That Test Day Feeling

Tests arouse a variety of feelings in students, including anxiety, as previously discussed. Work with them, individually and as a class, to identify and learn to control their test-inspired emotional reactions. In the following section, we provide several tools to develop productive test day feelings, including the Sample Attitude Survey in Figure 5.13.

Activity: Fishbowl Discussion Group

1. Have a group of four or five students, the "fishbowl" group, sit in the center of a larger circle of students. Each group has a unique task during this activity.

2. Fishbowl group: Choose a prompt to begin a discussion. Following are some possible prompts:
   - We take tests because _____.
   - I feel _____ the night before a test.
   - I feel _____ right before tests because _____.
   - During tests, I always feel _____.
   - I would enjoy tests more if _____.
   - Before tests, my parents always tell me to _____.
   - Before tests, my teacher usually tells me to _____.
   - I wish I could _____ to get ready for tests.
   - After tests, I feel _____.

FIGURE 5.12

How I Learn Best: Questionnaire

Ask yourself these questions:

- How do I learn?

- What are my favorite things to do?

- If I had a choice, how would I like to learn information?

Check your favorite ways to learn:

- ☐ Hearing it

- ☐ Seeing it

- ☐ Writing it down

- ☐ Working by myself

- ☐ Working with others

- ☐ Teaching it to someone else

- ☐ Creating it

- ☐ Talking about it

- ☐ Reading it

- ☐ Manipulating it

- ☐ Experiencing it

Summarize what you learned from the items you checked. Complete this sentence:

I learn best in the following ways: _____

_____.

FIGURE 5.13

Sample Attitude Survey

Before the tests, I feel _____

_____.

I need _____

_____ to make my scores higher on tests.

Tests frustrate me because _____

_____.

I enjoy tests because _____

_____.

My parents can help me prepare for a test by _____

_____.

My teacher can help me prepare for a test by _____

_____.

I would be more comfortable during tests if _____

_____.

I would enjoy celebrating completion of a test by _____

_____.

3. Outside group: First, record the fishbowl group's responses to the selected prompt; then, list two or three words to describe the fishbowl responses.

4. Whole group: Discuss the responses and ways to reduce test stress.

5. Other ways to use the prompts:
   - As a discussion cue in small groups, in conferences, or with the whole class
   - As journal entries
   - As attitudes probes on teacher-made tests or worksheets

Activity: My Many Colored Days

Read *My Many Colored Days* by Dr. Seuss. This book is filled with illustrations and metaphors to use in expressing feelings with colors. Each page can trigger excellent discussions on feelings and associations with any topic. For instance, ask students to complete the following activity on test day:

1. Choose a color that describes your test day feeling today: _____

2. Why did you choose that color? Discuss your response with a partner.

Activity: Posttest Feelings Questionnaire

Use this questionnaire after test sections for students to express feelings about their work.

The hardest part was _____.

The easiest part was _____.

The part that frustrated me most was _____.

Analyzing Your Performance

In addition to analyzing their feelings, students need to take a good look at their performance using Figure 5.14, After-the-Test Self-Check, or a similar tool. By using a critic's eye on their attitudes, behaviors, and strategies for test taking, they develop the self-awareness needed for improvement.

Action Lists

Action lists (Figure 5.15) and good test behaviors lists (Figure 5.16) remind students what to do before, during, and after tests. Post them

FIGURE 5.14

	Most of the Time	Often	Sometimes	Rarely If Ever
After-the-Test Self-Check				
1. Did I listen?				
2. Did I follow directions?				
3. Did I work independently?				
4. Did I pace myself?				
5. Did I use my time wisely?				
6. Did I complete the test on time?				
7. Did I study?				
8. Was I rested?				
9. Was I hungry or thirsty?				
10. Was I distracted?				
11. Did I understand the directions?				
12. Did I understand the questions?				
13. Did I have enough time to finish?				
14. Did I carefully check my work?				

A. If I had to take this test again, I would _____.

B. The hardest part of this test was _____.

C. The easiest part of this test was _____.

D. I want to tell you that I _____.

E. The next time I take a test, I will _____.

around the classroom as tests approach. Guide students in developing their own action lists as a class, in small groups, or individually. They may want to place the lists in their notebooks or take them home to post on refrigerators or in their study areas. Parents appreciate copies of action lists.

FIGURE 5.15

Action Lists

Before Test Day

Know the answer to these questions:
When is the test?
What kind of test is it?
How long is the test?
How do I need to review for it?
What memory hooks do I need to use?

Right Before the Test

Concentrate on the teacher's directions.
Mark important words in the directions.
Make yourself as comfortable as possible.

During the Test

Do
Pace yourself.
Answer the easiest questions first.
Mark the hardest questions to answer later.
Double-check your work.

Don't
Skip the directions.
Begin before the teacher tells you to start.
Make extra marks on the answer sheet.
Be concerned about your classmates.
Whisper to a friend.
Walk around during the test.

FIGURE 5.16

Good Test Behaviors List

In the Classroom
Listen to directions.
Focus on what is being said.
Ask questions about the test.

At Home
Ask your parents to help you get ready for the test.
Be proactive.
Prepare your materials and your mind.

Before the Test
Check your supplies.
Remove all distractions.
Clear your mind.

ALL YEAR: UNDERSTANDING THE VALUE OF PRACTICE

Students must be taught how to practice for tests. Follow the official test format for formal practice sessions, using the formal test guidelines and timing. Conduct these sessions as final rehearsals of a play. Many students participate in sports, music, or dance lessons. They spend hours practicing their skills. Foster the same dedication, enthusiasm, and spirit in academic practices. Adapt the following skit to emphasize the need for test practice.

A Ballpark View of Practicing: A Skit

Characters: Two students, Tommy and Anna

Props: Softball or baseball, bats, gloves, caps; for the scene in the kitchen, a student desk or table, two chairs, and test-taking materials (number two pencil, scratch pad, cover sheet, eraser, booklet)

Background Music (optional): "Take Me Out to the Ballgame"

The Play

As the scene opens, a player is leaving the ballpark following a big game (head down, walking slowly). Another player catches up and strolls along beside her.

Tommy: Hey, Anna. You look sick. What's wrong?

Anna: No, I'm not sick. I really tried to think about the game, but my mom and my teacher told me yesterday that I won't be able to play ball if I keep having trouble with my schoolwork. I sure don't want to miss our games, so I'm worried, Tommy. My class is getting ready for that long, hard test we have to take every year. I hate it. I get nervous every time I just hear somebody talk about it. I never do good work on tests. I'm afraid my scores will be low and I won't even get to come to practice.

Tommy: I know what you mean. We're getting ready for those tests in my class, too. I get so nervous I can't even think and my stomach feels like it's in knots. I have trouble remembering what we learned even when it's just for practice tests. Hey, Anna, I just thought of something. We never have a hard time thinking about practicing for our ball games, and we always remember what we are supposed to do. You would think I could keep my mind on a test since it doesn't last nearly as long as a game. I have a great idea!

Anna: What is it?

Tommy:	When I mentioned "practice," it made me think. We look forward to practicing before the games. Even when it's raining, we hope it will stop so we can practice. Let's see if we can think about getting ready for the test like we get ready for an important ballgame.
Anna:	Oh, I don't know, Tommy. I really like getting ready for every game. I don't ever want to miss one, but I sure want to miss that big test.
Tommy:	Let me think, Anna. Hmm. First, we should make a list of everything that would help us get ready for the game.
Anna:	That would be easy. Let's see if your mom will let you come over to my house for a while. Maybe you could eat pizza with us tonight. You can help me with my math, too. I already feel better. You know, Tommy, I don't believe I will ever feel as excited about any test as I am about a game, but it's worth a try.

Later, in the kitchen at Anna's house. The table has been cleared for the two students to work. Later in the scene, students will use test-taking materials, so they should be ready.

Tommy:	Okay, let's think about how Coach Warren gets us ready before our first game each year.
Anna:	Well, first we have to have our equipment. Then we get our schedules for practice sessions. We have many, many practices to learn how to catch and throw the ball, and to hit. I guess that's what the teacher is doing when we have questions like the ones that will be on the test.
Tommy:	The coach always tells us to keep our minds on the game. That's for sure.
Anna:	We sure do have to practice a lot. I'm beginning to feel better. But I still don't feel good about tests.
Tommy:	I know! Let's have a cheer like we do for our team. You know how we do our high fives, when we jump into the air and slap our hands together for good luck?
Anna:	Okay. Let's make up a cheer for the test.

The students work to create a test cheer. After some experimentation, they invent one: "Getting ready for a test just means doing your best!"

Anna:	Let's say it. Ready?
Both:	Getting ready for a test just means doing your best!
Anna:	I like cheers. What else do we need?
Tommy:	Well, the coach always tells us to eat good food and to get a lot of rest.

Anna: Right. And we have to be sure that we have all of our equipment for games, including our gloves.

Tammy and Anna pile up the test-taking materials on the table as Tommy talks.

Tommy: Yeah, and before the test, we have to be sure that we have everything we need, like a number two pencil, scratch paper, a cover sheet, a booklet, and an eraser.

Anna: We listen to all the instructions from our coach and remember to do everything he says.

Tommy: This is hard to believe—the teacher told us almost the same thing. She is always saying that we have to listen carefully and follow all the directions.

Anna: The coach tells us our positions, where to sit, when to go on the field, and how to act between innings. He teaches the plays, shows us all of the moves, and then has us practice them over and over.

Tommy: The teacher helps us learn all the information, practice it, and use it!

Anna: One of my favorite parts of the game is hearing our family and friends cheer and yell for us. That always makes us feel good. I know they can't be there to cheer when we take the test, but they can think about us and wish us good luck. That would make us feel better during the test.

Tommy: The coach always reviews the good and bad plays after the game. We always talk about how we played and how to improve. I hope our parents and the teacher show us our scores.

Anna: You know how the coach always reminds us just to do our best? This way of thinking about tests will help me. Tests are challenges just like our ballgames.

Curtain closes.

Extensions: A Ballpark View of Practicing

- Have students work in teams to write another scenario that compares practice for a performance with preparation for a test.
- Sing a "practice" song, such as the following:

I'm Ready for the Big Test

(To the tune of "Take Me Out to the Ball Game")

I'm ready for the big test.

I will give it my best.
My brain stored the important facts
I have easy "hooks" to bring them back.
I'll work, work, work through the whole test.
I'll use all things in my brain's store.
I know I will succeed using my best test tools
For a top test score!

ALL YEAR: SPARKING THE YEARNING FOR LEARNING

Before the achievement tests, a principal asked a class of fourth-grade students how they were feeling about the tests. One boy immediately responded with one word. He said, "Sick!" Later the boys and girls were asked how they felt during the test, and the same student's response was "Sick" (Kenny Hoff, fourth grader).

A second-grade teacher said, "On the morning of the first test day, my students acted as thought they had stage fright. They did not seem to remember anything we had practiced during the last few days. It was an extremely frustrating day for me" (Betsy Esa, second-grade teacher).

Desire is the key to learning. If the classroom excitement is strong and the way the material is presented is enticing, the student will be more likely to want to learn. However, individual desire, at the deepest level, must come from within. This "yearning to learn" must be in place for information to pass into the long-term memory banks.

Students need to have the "I can learn!" feeling. Each learner has areas of strength and can learn. Teachers must help students remove obstacles in their learning pathways.

Everyone in the learning community needs to exhibit belief in the student's abilities and be a cheerleader.

Testing and Meeting Basic Needs

There are preconditions to sparking the yearning to learn. People whose basic needs are unmet cannot attend to other matters, like test success. Students have physical and psychological needs that are comparable to those of adults. These human needs, as defined by Abraham Maslow, an American psychologist, can be located on an ascending hierarchy, with life's most basic needs on the lowest level (Bruno, 1992).

Physiological needs is the first level of the heirarchy. This includes food, clothing, and shelter. Students' physical needs must be recognized and met. A nutritious breakfast, healthy snacks, and plenty of rest are basic requirements. Classroom arrangements, room temperature, and the general environment must be comfortable and conducive to learning.

Safety and security is the second level. This is the need to be free from fear and to feel confident that physical needs will continue to be met. Fear of the unknown and fear of failure are prevalent prior to tests, with the result that the need for security is unmet. Teachers, administrators, and parents must provide a safe and secure environment.

The need to be social is the third level of the hierarchy. Using group projects to prepare for the test creates a team spirit. Setting class goals for success gives students a feeling of belonging.

The fourth level is the need for esteem. This includes self-esteem and recognition. Students who learn to use constructive, mature behaviors feel self-confident and in control. Students need opportunities to succeed in using test-taking skills. Encourage partner teams and small groups to use praise and self-affirmations.

The fifth level in Maslow's hierarchy is self-actualization. When a student reaches this level, the need for esteem is replaced with an innate desire "to be the best that I can be." When students learn how to be successful, they are more likely to achieve internal motivation and become self-actualized.

The most effective motivation is always self-motivation, the internal drive to do the best one can do. Learners need to understand the value of tests to cultivate a desire to do their best. They should know why it is important to remember the material they study. By seeing that what they do is valued, students learn to value their own learning. These feelings increase self-motivation.

The Effects of Expectations

One would not expect a student who has not done well on tests to do well in another testing situation. When people are not expected to do well, they usually do just what is expected. Past failure combined with low expectations from teachers, parents, and others hinders test performance.

The Pygmalion effect represents the opposite scenario in which the stage is set with high expectations. The students do well because they are expected to be successful. Students live up to the expectations of those around them, and nothing inspires like success. Just as applause makes actors forget the pain and drudgery of a production, encouragement and praise from the teacher, parents, and others. A sense of pride and self-fulfillment foster the desire to be successful on future tests.

One important way to set high expectations is by creating an upbeat, high-energy, supportive climate for testing. In the next chapter, we present ideas, strategies and activities to accomplish this goal.

Setting the Environment for Testing   **6**

When a child feels that his work is a task, it is only under compulsion that he gives himself to it. At every let up of external pressure this attention, released from constraint, flies to what interests him.

—John Dewey

THE SETTING

How would you describe the testing environment in your school and classroom? Is it comfortable, relaxed, positive, stimulating, exciting, and challenging? Would your students and their parents use these adjectives to describe the testing climate? If you answered yes to any of these questions, our hats are off to you. If, however, you answered no to any of these questions, you are probably in the majority. Just as in a stage play, in the testing scene, mood, and setting shape the performance. The testing scene must become interesting, comfortable, and challenging for students to enter into the state of flow—focused, enjoyable concentration—that is best for learning. (See also Chapman & King, 2008.)

Create an organized and inviting setting for testing. As in the theater, only when the appropriate props, sound, lighting, costumes, and other aspects of the environment are in place can the performance begin. We thoroughly investigated recent research into optimal learning (see Chapter 2). We reinforced our belief that brain-compatible learning environments for testing can be established, despite the negative mood that often surrounds the issue of testing. Our research is the foundation for the many practical ideas, guidelines, and suggestions presented here to design relaxed but stimulating and challenging test experiences. We hope you enjoy your role in creating the test scene!

PERSONALIZING THE ENVIRONMENT

Comfortable settings provide security and belonging. Students need to feel relaxed and at home in the classroom for effective learning to take place. Physical comfort and mental ease play major roles in performance. You might think of students' day-to-day learning environments as actors do their dressing rooms and rehearsal stages. These are comfortable, private, personal places free of external distractions where cast members can learn their roles for the big production. Most of all, it is backstage and during rehearsal that actors, members of the supporting crew, and the director come together and bond as a troupe. In the same way students, the teacher, school staff, and parents need to create strong bonds with activities focused on optimal learning and test success.

Create a sense of belonging by sharing tasks during test preparation. When learners assume responsibilities in the classroom and the school, they develop cohesiveness, ownership, and pride. They may assist by moving desks, covering instructional materials, sharpening pencils, posting "testing" banners and signs, and identifying obvious distractions such as the gerbil's squeaky wheel or the aquarium pump. Provide learning activities that create a team spirit and interpersonal support. This sense of community stimulates a desire to win or succeed.

After a test, have a Pep Rally, a Test Success Party, or a Grande Finale Jubilee to associate tests with pleasant experiences. Ask students what would make them more comfortable in various learning situations. Listen and act accordingly, if the suggestions are reasonable and feasible. Some students do their best work while stretched out on the floor. A cozy place to read may help others. Remember, you do not read your favorite book in a formal dining room chair.

Seeing a Familiar Face

The teacher's presence provides a great sense of security to students. In our opinion, it is unfortunate that some schools place other adults in the classroom to be the chief test administrators. The rationale is that the classroom teacher may influence or assist students with the test. An unknown test administrator, however, may create stress and anxiety for students. Even if you cannot be present during the test itself, during preparations, your familiar face can evoke a sense of comfort and security. In an ideal test situation, the teacher who is with the students during the majority of the day administers the test.

Familiarity also creates confidence. Familiarity with your class creates an open and encouraging atmosphere, which in turn improves students' self-confidence. Effective teachers become familiar with their students and use personal relationship tools, including compassion, understanding, and encouragement.

Using Humor

Laughter relaxes the mind, removes tension, builds rapport, and creates personal bonds. Humor has long been a tool of master teachers.

We are not suggesting, of course, that you become a comedian. But when you are able to laugh at yourself and share joy in living, students not only learn to use appropriate humor but also to deal with disappointment, embarrassment, and failure. Share humor in personal stories, jokes, riddles, and cartoons as another key to learning and test success.

Removing Barriers

Everyone should be asked to remain in their seats until all students have completed the test. Other people always complete the test before me. I am very intimidated and it makes me think about how slow I am. The movement and sound interfere with my concentration, too.

—Hilary, a college freshman

Ask students to identify barriers to test success and to describe problems. For example, a student may be intimidated when other students complete a test and are permitted to leave or move to other activities. The student's thinking process may be totally blocked by the distraction, causing unproductive reactions. To take care of this problem, you could have a simple rule stating that students should sit quietly until everyone completes the test or until the test session ends. Remind students to be aware of the barriers to concentration during informal and formal tests so each one can be discussed and new guidelines considered. A few common problems are discussed below.

Lighting

The type of lighting used in the classroom may not be an option; however, examine the room for lighting problems before tests. If the classroom has windows, check the light reflection on desks. A bright, dim, or blinking light can be distracting and interfere with vision. Even a small shadow may hinder concentration.

If feasible, use reading lamps to create a cozy atmosphere. Remember, too, that some students may be energized by light. Seat them near a bright natural or artificial light source.

Sounds

It is extremely difficult to provide a completely silent place for testing. Remember, however, that most students are accustomed to various noises during periods designated for quiet study. The complete absence of sound may be as distracting as unexpected noise.

Ask students to create a list of distracting sounds that may be heard during tests. Teach them how to refocus quickly after interruptions. Create distracting sounds occasionally during independent work, timed activities, and informal tests throughout the year. Blow a whistle loudly, or mumble, and then challenge students to stay on task. Record sounds to play occasionally during informal tests to rehearse the skill of refocusing on the task at hand. Sounds to record include sneezes, motors, sirens, voices, and intercom announcements. See "Tuning Out Distractions" on page 86.

Provide time for students to discuss how they would cope with the distractions. It helps to hear how classmates would handle each situation. Have students make journal entries related to appropriate reactions to the distractions.

Air Circulation

Cool, fresh air is conducive to proper brain functioning. Stagnant air causes drowsiness. If possible, open a window to bring in fresh air. Use a fan, if needed, but be sure the students have worked previously with a fan blowing and that the fan noise is not distracting.

Before a test or during transitions, take brisk, short walks outside if possible. The air and movement will refresh and energize the mind.

Temperature

Air that is too cool or too warm creates discomfort. When air temperature is too warm, drowsiness results. Any discomfort interferes with thinking. Unfortunately, though, classroom temperature is usually controlled by a central system. During testing, maintain the same temperature used throughout the year if possible. Sudden changes in temperature are distracting. If the classroom's temperature cannot be controlled or predicted, tell students to wear layers of clothing, so they can put on or take off a sweater or jacket.

Arranging the Scene

On the day of the test, a little girl started to cry when the teacher began to move her desk. The teacher hugged the student and asked why she was so upset. The girl replied through tears, "The sun won't shine on my desk over there. I can't work without the sun shining on my desk!"

Desks are usually rearranged before a major test to reduce distractions and deter cheating. Students need to be accustomed to new desk placements before the formal test. The incident with the little girl who needed the sun on her desk occurred in a second-grade classroom as the desks were being moved on the first morning of a standardized test. To prevent a problem such as this one, move student desks occasionally during regular tests to simulate the formal testing atmosphere. When students are taught to move the desks, they can make quick scene changes. This task may be accomplished "Quickly and Quietly," or Q&Q. Give students a voice in arranging the room for test day. Ask where they would work best during the test. Some prefer working at a table or on the floor rather than at a desk. Give all students the opportunity to find the best spot for concentration, where they will be comfortable and not bother or be bothered by anyone else. Allow students to give input, but remember that you must follow all testing guidelines and make the final decisions.

On the stage, actors and the director work together to arrange carefully how the characters will sit, stand, and move during the scene. The actors need to become comfortable with the arrangement before opening night. Take the same care in arranging the classroom or other testing environment for test day.

Creating Privacy

A lack of privacy can disrupt the test experience. Students lacking in confidence may be tempted to look for answers on classmates' answer sheets or booklets, if answers are visible. Even the best students become distracted when they are aware that a classmate is looking at their paper or even looking their way. But when each student's work area cannot be seen by others, cheating need not concern the teacher or students.

Create a privacy fence or cubicle for a desk or work area by folding a large piece of heavy-duty cardboard into three parts. Place the screen on a desk or table to provide privacy. The dividers may be personalized with special designs. Introduce the cubicles early in the year during regular activities and informal tests to be sure the novelty wears off. Do not use these privacy dividers for the first time during a formal test. With experience, each student will discover if the divider improves or hinders concentration. Some students enjoy the isolation, while others need an open work area. Allow individual students to decide if they want to use a cubicle.

CREATING HYPE FOR THE PRODUCTION

Actors keep personal photos, mementos, and good luck charms in their dressing rooms. Costumes, props, and posters advertising the play remind performers that the big performance is coming. All of these items generate anticipation and excitement. Students also benefit from efforts to make the test setting personal, fun, exciting, and special.

Signs

Use kind, humanistic terms on classroom signs (see Figure 6.1). The traditional "Do Not Disturb" reminders have negative connotations. Communicate the same message using positive, catchy phrases to deter intrusions during test periods. For example, drape a bright yellow or orange caution ribbon across the classroom door with a phrase written in a positive tone.

FIGURE 6.1 Sample Signs
Caution: Brains at Work
—Danger: Testing Zone—
Brain Drain in Progress!
Doing Our Best on the Test
Knowledge Explosion in Progress
★★Testing What We Know: Now Showing★★
Test Production in Process

Cheering the Way

Bulletin boards, banners, posters, door displays, and mobiles make colorful, eye-catching test success reminders (see Figure 6.2). Design the visuals to surround students in a positive atmosphere.

FIGURE 6.2	Sample Slogans for Bulletin Boards, Banners, Charts, and Posters

Show What You Know

—Giving it Your Best Shot—

YOU KNOW IT! JUST DO IT!

Flower Power

Using My Eagle Eye

The Test: A Drain for Your Brain!

★★★ Test Ready ★★★

Bright Ideas!

TEST SUCCESS MEANS DOING MY BEST

Smiley Chain

This display involves all the students and adults in the school! Everyone creates a smiley face with his or her name on it. Connect the faces to form a chain. Attach the chain to a banner that reads "Test Ready." Display the Smiley Chain so it is seen by everyone.

Students in the upper grades can write adjectives or phrases in a graffiti way to create a chain.

Use Special Props

Because tests can be extremely discouraging, students need to know that their efforts are valued. As students prepare for the test, generate excitement and a sense of accomplishment by providing motivating props. The Genius Jar and other activities we describe here help learners feel good about each small success with tests.

Genius Jar

This activity teaches students that they do many things well.

1. Obtain a large, clear jar and label it "Genius Jar" in a graffiti way. Paste the names of all students on the outside of the jar.

2. Place small strips of paper next to the Genius Jar. Note: Cut the paper strips large enough for one or two to fit inside the jar and keep a supply near the container.

3. After each test, students respond to the question "What did I do well on the test?" They write the response on one side of a strip of paper and their name on the other side.

4. Tell students to place each Smart Strip in the Genius Jar.

5. Before the next test, use the Smart Strips as a review of test-taking skills and test success. Call on individual students to take out one Smart Strip at a time and read the response and the author's name. Celebrate by giving a thumbs-up or high fives.

Variation: Cut a large jar shape out of paper for a bulletin board display with each student's name fanning out from the top of the jar. Place the Smart Strips on and around the Genius Jar.

Brag Bag

Use this activity in the middle of test week.

1. Give each student a paper "Brag" bag.

2. Ask students to create a self-portrait on the front of the bag.

3. Tell them to place words that describe their feelings and reactions to tests around the picture.

4. Ask students to label one side of the bag "Likes" and the opposite side"Dislikes." On the "Like" side, tell them to write what they enjoy about tests and the test skills they find easy to use. On the "Dislike" side, tell them to record test skills they find difficult to use.

5. Write prompts for student responses on simple cutout shapes, such as circles or squares, and place them inside the bag. Prompt examples include the following:
   • My best test skill is _____.
   • I need to remember to _____.
   • During the test, I felt good about _____.

6. Form a conversation circle and have students share and discuss items from their Brag Bags.

Cool Test Kit

A Cool Test Kit designed by students generates pleasant feelings to connect with testing experiences. Make the kit from a box, can, sack, or other suitable container. Students may personalize the kits by giving them a unique name, using colorful artwork, and selecting personally meaningful supplies to place inside the kit. Use the kits in formal and informal testing throughout the year.

Names for the kits include the following:

- Lucky Bucket
- Tackle Box
- Power Pail
- Bright Bags
- Swell Pail
- Toolbox
- Smart Sack

Items students may place in the kit include the following:

- Extra pencils
- Scratch paper
- Eraser
- "Sticky" notes to mark "rethink" test items
- A test "pet," such as a pet rock
- Snacks such as food bars, raisins, mint, candy, gum
- A favorite picture or drawing
- A water bottle
- Encouraging notes from someone special
- A small mirror to view the most important person in the test scene
- Tissues
- Lucky symbols or charms

Cool School Tools

Give special names related to testing to pencils, notepads, and rulers, using logos with special names to encourage and promote thinking. A Smart Pencil is a popular example. Logos to place on pencils and other tools include the following:

Zap the Test
Doing My Best on the Test
Test Zest
Rock Steady . . . I'm Test Ready

MOTIVATING THE CAST

A team spirit energizes the class and creates group bonds. When students realize that their performance on each test contributes to a total class score, they are likely to put forth more effort. Here are a few tips to create a motivating environment for your cast:

- Compare the test to a game, such as the school's biggest sporting event of the year. Remind students that standardized tests are designed to reflect their abilities as individuals and as a group in the same way a game demonstrates the ability of each player and the team. Each person contributes to the team's total score. In this metaphor, the players are the students; the coaches and fans are the teachers, staff, parents, other relatives, neighbors, and friends. Create a team name based on the teacher's name: "The Gillespie Gang" or "Bradshaw's Bunch" or other special, descriptive words.
- Employ the stage metaphor used throughout this book to illustrate the value of individual work and group success. Stress the value of each performer's role in test success.
- Use the ideas provided in this chapter to design special events and decorations for the test.
- Brainstorm other possible events and decorations with students.

PRETEST CELEBRATIONS

The purpose for testing is to assess information learned. Learning is a phenomenal process to celebrate often. Design celebrations to create a spirit for test success. Celebrations also bring attention to the school's value of high student achievement. Use the following suggestions and activities in your classroom or throughout the school to create a team spirit and foster high expectations.

Activities for the Classroom

Before a testing period, generate excitement and confidence by implementing these intriguing activities. Adapt the ideas provided here for your classroom.

Grand Openings

Hold a ribbon-cutting ceremony to signify the opening day for a test week. Invite parents and special guests to attend. Share jingles, poems, songs, and raps to promote test success.

Test Shower

Have a party to mark the impending event. Invite parents to send notes that show their pride in how much has been learned. Share and post these good luck messages.

Cheers, Raps, and Banner Themes

Engage students in creating cheers, raps, and themes for banners, bulletin boards, mobiles, and posters. Add colorful illustrations to bring attention and meaning to displays. Examples include the following:

- Cheers

  Go for the Gold!
  Going for Our Test Best!

- Raps

  We will . . . we will . . . do our best!
  We will zap this test!
  Rock Steady! We Are Test Ready!

- Banner Themes

  Giving Our Best to the Test
  Soar With a High Test Score
  Winners Do Their Best

Cross-Age Tutoring

Older students who have experienced test success provide excellent role models for younger students. Use test buddies to develop positive attitudes and good test strategies.

- Share strategies and tips for test success in small groups.
- Have students cowrite poems, raps, banners, signs, and jingles.
- Present skits to demonstrate the correct way to take tests.
- Challenge younger students to "walk through" their thinking processes verbally on parts of a practice test, with a test buddy giving feedback.

Schoolwide Celebrations

School décor can create excitement before major tests. Reinforce a positive testing spirit in the classroom, in the hallways, and during special schoolwide events.

Prepare the School for the Performance

Decorate the school entrance, special areas, hallways, wings, and doorways with motivating logos, sayings, and words of encouragement. Give students opportunities to create banners, mobiles, posters, and signs to communicate high expectations for test success.

Adapt the following example for schoolwide testing.

Decorated Door Celebrations

During the week before the testing begins, assign a school door to a class or a group of students and an adult supervisor. Select a theme similar to the following ideas to generate excitement for the upcoming test event.

- A slogan for doing well on the test
- Content information students need to know for the test
- Test-taking strategies

After the doors are complete, guide the students on supervised walks or scavenger hunts to read and discuss the displayed information related to their future test-taking adventure.

Fanfares and Publicity

- Release colorful helium balloons with Test Ready logos on the playground.
- Have all students and staff write to someone on the Web in another country, state, city, district, or school about the test celebration.
- Publicize the school's test-spirit message and the Test Ready theme through local media.
- Post flyers or student-made posters related to test celebrations in local businesses, stores, offices, and malls.

- Use the intercom or closed-circuit television for students to present an instrumental piece, rap, poem, song, or jingle to open each test day.
- Have student representatives and teachers talk to local civic groups and organizations about the new view of tests as learning celebrations.

Sing-Alongs

Conduct a schoolwide sing-along over the intercom before each test day begins. Choose a song such as "I'm Great and Getting Greater" to generate energy and enthusiasm for the test. Pass out a copy of the words to the song to give everyone time to learn the lines before the sing-along. Invite everyone in the school to participate.

I'm Great and Getting Greater

The following words are from Carolyn Chapman's CD, *Making the Shoe Fit.* The lyrics were written by Connie Ryals. Copy the lyrics and use them as poems or raps.

> *Life's a journey every day*
> *No matter what your age*
> *You can learn something new*
> *Just believe today's the day*
> *You can learn a foreign language or play a saxophone*
> *You can go and climb a mountain or write a novel of your own*

(Refrain)

> *We're great and getting greater*
> *You're great and getting greater*
> *I'm great and getting greater each day*
> *We're great and getting greater*
> *You're great and getting greater*
> *I'm great and getting greater each day*
> *You turn to me, I turn to you*
> *You say to me, and I say to you, too,*
> *That we're great and getting greater*
> *You're great and getting greater*
> *I'm great and getting greater every day.*
>
> *Don't look back from where you've come*
> *But just learn from things you've done*

Every day is like brand new
with the rising of the sun
Look ahead, the new horizon
is waiting there it's true
Come celebrate the life you've been given
'Cause you're the only you.

Spirit Week

Try the following activities during a dedicated Spirit Week:

- Share rewards or recognition received from previous test scores.
- Wear school colors.
- Select songs that reflect celebrations and success, such as the theme from the movie *Rocky,* "Celebrate," or "I Can See Clearly Now."
- Repeat the slogan "Giving Our Best on the Test" as a school test rap.
- Have students create and perform test raps, jingles, and songs.
- Pep rallies create hype for the big event—the test! Each class or grade level may design and present its own cheers, banners, raps, jingles, and songs.
- Plant a tree or flower in honor of test success. Give the plant a name.
- Bury a time capsule in the fall. Ask students to project their learning success for the year and to include lucky charms and symbols that encourage them to achieve their goals. They can add special drawings or pictures of people and things that will help them be successful during the year. Open the capsule on the day prior to the test.

Test Play

Several days prior to the big test, organize mock tests or test-related events to communicate a fun, relaxed atmosphere. The following activities provide opportunities for students to associate the term *test* with positive experiences through familiar games and activities.

1. Taste Test

   Step One: Place an unusual food sample in a small paper cup or doily and put it on each student's lunch tray. Choose foods that are not eaten by most students, such as tapioca, kiwis, avocados, and beets.

   Step Two: Instruct students to rate the sample taste on a classroom chart over the course of a week.

Step Three: Compile the charted results at the end of the week.

Step Four: Post the results for everyone to view.

2. Physical Tests
   - Use noncompetitive sports to test strength, endurance, and other physical abilities.
   - Participate in a student or teacher tug-of-war, relay race, or obstacle course.
   - Involve all members of the community of learners, including administrators, custodians, cafeteria staff, parents, specialists, and classroom teachers.

Music Tests

- Play name that tune to test song recognition.
- Use matching games to test knowledge of instruments, types of music, composers, or note recognition.
- Play music bingo with the facts or terminology.

Library Tests

- Match authors to poems, books, and stories.
- Match pictures to the illustrator.
- Match characters to movies, nursery rhymes, and stories.

Test-Ready Fling

- Organize a day of cooperative games such as water balloon tosses, obstacle courses, relay races, or other challenging activities.

Supporting Roles: Help for the Crew

Community members and organizations, parents and parent groups, and the school administrators can pitch in to make test events special. Their contributions show students how valuable their learning accomplishments are to the whole community.

Sponsored Free Breakfast

- Provide a free breakfast for all students on the first test day! This celebrates the test and encourages students to arrive at school early, too. Ask a school sponsor to provide the breakfast or a portion of the meal. Invite parents to attend the breakfast to give the students their show of support on this first important day in the test week.

- As vehicles arrive on the first day of a major test week, give each driver and student a healthy breakfast bar or treat.

Parent-Sponsored Smart Carts

The school's parent organization can show its support by serving nutritional snacks and juice.

- Serve healthy snacks on a cart labeled "Smart Cart."
- Enjoy the snacks before the test or during transitions.
- Discuss the value of foods for producing energy and brain power.
- If weather permits, allow students to take their snacks and go for a walk to a special place outside.

Antics From the Principal

The principal sets the tone for the school's test success. The leader's enthusiasm and high expectations energize the entire student body. Students enjoy and bond with the principal who participates in entertaining events as learning celebrations. The activities build rapport and communicate the administrator's expectations for test success.

Use the line: "Get the principal to _____! Do your best on the test!" Fill in the blank with any of these suggested antics or others of your own invention:

- Kiss a pig.
- Spend time on the roof.
- Wear a clown costume all day.
- Sport a special haircut/shaved head.
- Be the dunce in a dunking machine.

INTERMISSIONS/TRANSITIONS

Design the intermissions, transitions, or the time between tests to renew students physically and mentally. Avoid having students spend transition time in their test seats. Movement and fresh air during transitions enhance optimal functioning of the brain.

Effective Transitions

Use the following suggestions to take advantage of time between test sections to recharge students' mental and physical batteries.

Letting Students React to the Test

When a test section is completed and time permits, ask for questions and concerns. Students need to express general reactions to the test. Keep conversations upbeat; show your belief in students' test-taking abilities. Here are some sample questions:

- What were the trickiest or hardest problems?
- How was your pacing? Did you complete the test before the time expired?
- What was your most useful test-taking strategy?
- What can you do to improve on the next part of the test?

Quiet Time

Provide a brief quiet time immediately before each test session to set the tone for the next segment. Use this time to remind students to check their supplies, such as pencils, erasers, and booklets, needed for the upcoming test session.

Other Transition Activities

Use transition activities throughout the year during informal assessment and between classes. Relaxing activities recharge the brain. Try some of these ideas.

- Repeat energizing team cheers.
- Listen to relaxing music.
- Use Cool Test Kits or Lucky Buckets.
- Sharpen pencils.
- Share pep notes from teacher, parents, and peers.
- Sing favorite class songs, repeat jingles, or read poems or raps.
- Participate in movement activities or take a brisk walk outside.
- Play a round of a favorite class game.

CLOSING CELEBRATIONS

The time following a major test provides an excellent opportunity for administrators, teachers, and parents to congratulate students for their concentration, hard work, and test success. Invite everyone who encouraged and supported students to the celebrations.

Activities for the Classroom

As the testing director, it is your job, with the help of the cast and crew, to celebrate the successful conclusion of the test. Here are some ideas for posttest events.

Cast Parties

Hold an ice cream, pizza, or popcorn party as a reception for cast and supporters.

A Piece of Cake

Serve a piece of cake to each student to celebrate the class test slogan, "Testing...a piece of cake." (Idea contributed by Olivia Moore, ESL teacher, Pearland, Texas.)

Energizing Cheers

Give partners, small groups, or the whole team special cheers like these:

- Microwave: Move the little finger in a waving motion while saying, "Great job."
- Round of applause: Continuously clap hands while moving them in a complete circle.
- Seal of approval: Clap backs of hands together while making the sound of a seal.
- High fives: Pairs of students hit opposite hands together high in the air above their heads while saying, "Yes!"

Variation: Give students opportunities to create and personalize cheers.

A Pat on the Back

1. Draw an outline of your own hand on construction paper. Cut it out so you can use it as a pattern.

2. Use the pattern to draw a "hand" for each student. Cut out each one.

3. Write "A Pat on the Back" on one side of each hand and sign it.

4. Place the hand on each student's back. Later, encourage them to place the "hand" on their desk as a reminder of your support.

Whole-School Celebrations

Adapt the ideas presented earlier for whole-school celebrations, such as fanfares, sing-alongs, and community- or parent-sponsored food treats, as celebrations after the test. Consider holding posttest field days, storytelling days, or special craft-making events. The principal can sponsor whole-school versions of classroom celebrations, such as cast parties, a piece of cake, cheers, and a pat on the back, as well as Olympic-style closing ceremonies, parades, or test "homecoming" events.

TEACHERS SET THE MOOD

A student asked, "Teacher, do you like me?" The teacher quickly responded, "Sure I do."

The student quipped, "Well, why don't you tell your face?"

Just as on the stage, in the classroom, tone of voice, facial expression, and body language communicate as much or more than the words spoken. The teacher's classroom presence sets the tone for all student experiences, including testing. Teachers have the power to create exciting atmospheres for testing. When students are led to view each test as a challenge and celebration of learning, healthy emotional attitudes develop.

Directors must create the right mood and setting for audiences to appreciate the play. They foster a team spirit among cast and crew to encourage the best possible performance. As the testing director, you have an equally challenging, and rewarding, set of tasks as you create the mood and setting necessary for top test performance. After opening night, all members of the cast and crew need to evaluate their performance. As the testing director, you need to take some time to analyze your own performance, too. Use the checklist below.

Teacher Performance Checklist

☐ Achieved and communicated a positive attitude before the test.
☐ Asked quality questions.
☐ Established a positive climate.
☐ Minimized distractions.
☐ Did my best to teach test-taking strategies.
☐ Made supportive comments throughout the process.

Teachers touch eternity. You never know where their influence stops.

—Henry B. Adams

Test-Taking Skills 7 and Strategies

A grandmother asked her grandson, a first grader, what he thought about his first day of achievement tests. He said, "Grandma, it was easy, but when I finished I remembered you told me to check my work and I kept thinking Grandma told me to check my work when I finished. I kept thinking about it, but I didn't know what check meant, so I just got out my book and started reading."

—Braden, a first grader

WHY TEACH TESTING STRATEGIES?

Many times educators assume students understand how to use seemingly obvious test-taking terms and strategies. For example, why should students intuitively know what *check your work* means? The reality is that they need to be taught the vocabulary and tricks associated with test skills and strategies, just as they need instruction in content areas.

This chapter provides a primer on how to teach some of the most important skills students need on the test day. We have noticed that many students have the knowledge base they need to do well on a test but lack strategies to approach the mechanics of answering multiple-choice questions, from knowing how to narrow down possible answers to using time wisely. For instance, we share activities to teach the simple but crucial skill of bubbling in, or marking the answer to each test question in a way scoring machines can read correctly.

On test day, you cannot assist a student with a difficult question, just as a director cannot leap onto the stage. Each performer, on this day, is alone on stage. In the same way that the actors internalize the director's advice through practice and rehearsal, learners of all ages must internalize an understanding of test terms and formats. And you must empower them with a variety of strategies to apply as they prepare for and take tests.

These skills cannot be internalized in the day or week before a test; the weeks before the major test are not the time to teach students how to approach questions. To ensure top performance on test day, introduce, teach, and practice each test-taking strategy using current content throughout the school year. Make these experiences exciting. Use stimulating instructional activities and interesting content information to practice or review materials so students look forward to learning the secrets of unlocking the answers. Use mysteries, problem-solving puzzles, brainteasers, and other game formats to teach students how to take a test and review vital information in all content areas. Make a commitment to yourself to make these teaching sessions exciting and stimulating for your students' minds. Scores will improve when test takers are trained, over time and with practice, to think like test makers and test-taking experts.

In this chapter, we explore more complex thinking skills to "attack the problem" presented in test directions. Students use higher-order thinking skills throughout the year as they tackle a variety of learning tasks, and they are crucial for success on test day.

ELEMENTS OF THE STRATEGIES IN THIS CHAPTER

We organized each strategy in the next two chapters to include the following elements:

- The Purpose section explains each test-taking strategy in simple, practical terms that can be communicated to students, so they will understand why they need to know the skill.
- The How To section provides the basic steps of the strategy.
- The Applications in the Real World section gives examples of everyday situations to show students how the strategies are meaningfully connected to their daily lives.
- The Early Grades and Upper Grades sections feature skill-related activities targeted for different age groups. These activities can become an integral part of the curriculum for all ages and grade levels, including learners with special needs. The lower grade activities may be adapted for upper grade learners. Students who learn many pathways to solutions become test-wise, independent learners.
- The Self-Talk section encourages students to plan, monitor, and evaluate their use of each strategy by providing questions to ask themselves and motivational statements to use as affirmations.

Skills and Strategies Covered in This Chapter

Tuning In: Using and following oral directions

Following Written Directions: Learning to read, interpret, and do

Bubbling In: Learning to fill in the answer sheet quickly and accurately

Know and Go: Learning to trust your instincts about an answer and move on

Bee Back: Learning to answer easy questions first and mark difficult ones to revisit later

When in Doubt, Try It Out! Learning to make educated guesses

Take a Double Take: Check, Check, Check! Learning to check your work and avoid careless errors

Set the Pace: Learning to control the time spent on each task

Keep On Keeping On: Learning to try different approaches and be persistent

TUNING IN

Purpose

- To listen for rules
- To listen for directions
- To hear the time limits

How To

1. Be alert for a cue to begin listening.

2. Stop what you are doing.

3. Look at the speaker.

4. Tune in to the directions. If permitted, jot down the key words in the directions on scratch paper.

5. Concentrate. Focus. Listen.

6. Look at the speaker.

7. Visualize yourself in the picture, listening.

8. Do not do other things.

9. Form questions.

10. Follow the directions.

Applications in the Real World

- Listening to directions may keep you from becoming lost.
- Being a good listener could save your life in an emergency situation.
- Listening to the coach will increase individual and team success.
- Being a good listener shows respect for the speaker.

Early Grades

Reminder Jar

Remind students of the "Say It One Time" rule, placing a button, coin, or other manipulative in a jar each time someone asks for a direction or statement to be repeated. Use this in a positive way as a reminder of this important listening skill.

Directed Designs

1. Instruct students to place X's on the grid to create a design, following oral directions. For example, tell students, "Place an X on A1. Place an X on E1. Place an X on B2," and so on. (See Figure 7.1.)

2. Students create their own design by plotting the symbols.

3. A classmate then draws the design using the creator's oral directions.

Variation: Play Simon Says as an exercise in following oral directions.

FIGURE 7.1

	1	2	3	4	5
A	X				X
B		X		X	
C			X		
D		X		X	
E	X				X

Memory Tag

1. Have four or five designated memory spots.

2. Tell students to listen to the directions so they know what to do in each spot to be "safe," such as sit with legs crossed, do jumping jacks, or hop on one foot.

3. If tagged, the students must perform a task, such as repeat a jingle, complete a series of exercises, or repeat a tongue twister.

Ball Recall

1. Ask each student to write five items in a selected category.

2. The students bring their personal lists and form a circle.

3. The teacher bounces the ball to a student.

4. The ball holder reads one item and bounces the ball to another student.

5. This learner recalls the stated item. One item on his or her own list is read, and the ball is bounced to another classmate who recalls the items read and adds one.

6. If the items are recalled correctly, the student bounces the ball to someone else. If the list is recalled incorrectly, the ball is returned to the classmate to repeat the list and bounce the ball to another student.

Upper Grades

Back to Back

1. Form A and B partners. Sit back to back.

2. Place a mat, tray, or cookie sheet in front of each student.

3. Give each partner a set of matching manipulatives or items such as pebbles, marbles, shells, or tokens.

4. Student A arranges the items in a design on the tray.

5. Student A then instructs Student B to place the objects on her tray to create the same design. Student B cannot talk or ask questions.

6. When each participant completes the design, they turn to face each other and compare them.

7. They discuss instructions that worked best and agree on what would make it easier to follow the directions the next time.

8. A and B change roles and repeat the activity using a different design.

9. This time Student A can ask questions, which receive only yes or no responses from Student B. Otherwise, follow the same procedure.

Say It One Time

1. Establish the precedent of saying directions only one time.

2. Use the "Say It One Time" slogan on banners, posters, and announcements.

Origami

Use a book on the Japanese craft of origami to teach listening skills for directions. Following oral directions, the students learn to make shapes, animals, or flowers and hone their test-taking skills.

Self-Talk

- Do I know exactly what I need to do?
- Did I listen to every detail?
- Is there anything else that I need to know ?
- I need to put what was said in my own words.
- What do I need to jot down or highlight to help me remember?

FOLLOWING WRITTEN DIRECTIONS

Purpose

- To know what to do
- To know steps and procedures
- To understand your task
- To gather instructions

How To

1. Read all directions thoroughly and carefully.

2. Check, highlight, underline, or circle the words that tell you what to do. Example: Take notes here, continue, go to the next page, stop.

3. Number the directions.

4. Visualize the steps.

5. When the task is completed, go over the directions again to see if you followed them correctly.

Applications in the Real World

- Learning a new game
- Following recipes
- Taking medication correctly
- Paying bills

Early Grades

Words in Action

1. Identify unfamiliar words learners will encounter on the test in written directions.

2. Write each word on a card.

3. Students create actions for each direction word.

4. A parade is formed with students acting out their words. Examples of action words to use for the parade include the following: *write, underline, draw, circle, divide, color,* and *match.*

Variation: Create a bulletin board to show test directions written as road signs, using the action words.

Signs and Actions

1. The teacher identifies words the learners will encounter in written directions. Examples: *Illustrate, underline,* and *summarize.*

2. Students form partners or triad teams.

3. The teacher shows the word and reads it.

4. Each group comes to consensus on a definition and action to demonstrate the word. They each write down the word and their definition.

5. The teacher names a word and calls on groups to perform the action and state the meaning.

Note: Continue to add words to the list throughout the year. Display the words with the students' meanings.

React to the Facts

Ask students to fold a sheet of paper into four sections and to use one section to complete a direction. Supply written directions. Here are some suggestions:

1. Draw a box with star and five dots inside.
2. Add the day of your birth four times.
3. Write your age four times and find the sum.
4. Write your full name. Circle the vowels. Underline the consonants.

Upper Grades

Step by Step

Tell students you are going to hand out a set of directions. Instruct them to read *all* directions carefully before they begin. This is extremely important for success on all tests. Example:

1. When you complete all directions, draw pictures of your favorite things in each corner and in the margins of your paper.
2. Write your name in the lower left-hand corner.
3. Draw a stick figure in the lower right-hand side.
4. Write the name of your favorite actor in the center of your paper.
5. Write your telephone number on the left margin.
6. Draw a star in the upper left-hand corner.
7. Write the name of your favorite food at the bottom of your paper.
8. Smile! You have almost completed this task.
9. Only complete direction #2 and pretend that you are working.

Mystery Numbers

Students read and follow directions to discover the mystery number.

1. Take the number of inches in a foot (12).
2. Add the number of feet in a yard (3).
3. Subtract the number of fingers on your left hand (5).
4. Multiply by the number of pints in a quart (2).

The answer is 20.

1. Take the day of the month for Independence Day (4).

2. Multiply that number by the number of angles in a triangle (3).

3. Subtract the number in half a dozen (6).

4. Add the number of months in the year (12).

The answer is 18.

Self-Talk

- I read all the directions. Now what did they tell me to do?
- I looked for key words in the directions.
- Did I follow each step?
- I'll read the directions again see if I did everything I was told to do.

BUBBLING IN

Purpose

- To know how to fill in a small circle correctly that matches the right answer for each question, using a number two pencil
- To be sure the test is scored accurately
- To allow you to show what you know

How To

1. Use a number two pencil.

2. Using the hand you do not write with, point to the correct answer on your test booklet so you don't lose your place.

3. Use the other hand to fill in the bubble next to the correct number on your answer sheet.

4. Completely fill in the bubble with the lead of your number two pencil.

5. Stay inside the bubble while filling in.

6. Erase all marks outside the bubble.

Applications in the Real World

- Coloring inside the lines in a coloring book
- Completing driver's license and college entrance exams
- Filling out job applications

Early Grades

Quick Activity Ideas

- Host a bubble-blowing bonanza with bubble soap to examine and discuss different sizes of bubbles.
- Color sheets of circles to practice staying inside the lines.
- Create and post a chart of rules to avoid "Bubble Trouble."

Mr. Bubble Cop

Mr. Bubble Cop is a character who teaches students how to do the following:

- Fill in bubble response formats.
- Build individual speed and accuracy when bubbling in.
- Avoid stray marks.
- Make corrections.
- Be sure the number of the item and the number of the bubble match.

Making Mr. Bubble Cop

1. Draw circles on dark construction paper.

2. Cut out the circles on the lines.

3. Glue the circles together to create the Bubble Cop character.

4. Display the designs during tests as a reminder to "Beware of Bubble Trouble."

5. Have students learn the poem "Mr. Bubble Cop's Rules."

   ### Mr. Bubble Cop's Rules

   Let Mr. Bubble Cop remind you

   To use a pencil number two.

   Stay in the lines. Now do it just right!

   Fill in the circle with all your might.

Use a finger to keep your place,
Mark the bubble in the right space.
Erase all the extra marks you make,
Avoid Bubble Trouble for Pete's sake!

Note: Remember that upper-grade students also need to increase their speed and accuracy with filling in bubbles.

Upper Grades

Perfect Penny Prints

1. Place a penny under a thin piece of paper.

2. Use a number two pencil. Rub the pencil point over the penny without making a mark outside the penny's edge.

3. Use a timer to see how many Perfect Penny Prints are made in a set time limit. Repeat with a lower time limit.

Variations: Use other coins or flat, circular objects.

Black Dot Mystery

1. Draw a circle and shade it in with a number-two pencil.

2. Write a mystery story, rap, chant, or song about the black dot that teaches the rules to remember about bubbling in on the test.

Self-Talk

- Did I follow the rules for bubbling in?
- Are all circles filled in completely?
- Are all unnecessary marks erased?
- Did I stay out of bubble trouble?

KNOW AND GO

Purpose

- To recognize the "aha" or intuitive feeling when you know the answer. Your first thought is usually right.

- To learn to mark the answer quickly and move on
- To avoid analyzing a question too much

How To

1. Read the question.

2. Read the answers.

3. If you know one answer is right, mark it.

4. If you *know* it, do not change your answer.

5. Move to the next question.

Applications in the Real World

- Responding in an emergency
- Changing tactics midplay in sports
- Choosing to buy something at a one-day sale
- Making the next move in a board, card, or computer game

Early Grades

Know and Go Rap

When you know the answer is right
Mark it and put it out of sight!
Then keep on the go
Find the next one you know.

Quick Pick

1. Divide students into teams.

2. Give each team ten index cards, each containing a multiple-choice problem.

3. When the teacher says "Quick Pick," a team member draws a problem card and reads it. After a discussion, the team comes to consensus on an answer and writes it on a separate piece of paper or answer sheet.

4. Give a short time to answer. The problem card is put aside when the team has an answer.

5. When the teacher says "Quick Pick" again, a team member draws another problem card.

6. Provide the answer key. The team with the greatest number of correct answers wins.

Variation: Write the multiple-choice problems on a PowerPoint program or SMART Board.

Upper Grades

Moving on Down Rap

Study it

Decide

Mark it

Move on!

Base Race

1. Develop a set of questions from material to be tested.

2. Form two teams, A and B, and have each team line up in single file.

3. Mark a starting line and a finish line.

4. The first member of each team will race to cross the finish line.

5. Read a question and display responses in a multiple-choice format.

6. The first student to cross the line has the first opportunity to select the correct response to the question.

7. If the first student to cross the line fails to answer correctly, the other team's runner has a chance.

8. Give a point for a correct answer.

9. The next two students step up to the starting line, and the game continues.

Team Choice

- Create cooperative teams with three or four members.
- Give each team four blank cards and one dark, broad-tipped marker.
- Give the teams the following directions:

  1. Write one letter, *A, B, C,* or *D,* on each card in large, dark print.

2. Tell the students that you will display a question with four possible answers that are labeled *A, B, C,* and *D.*

3. Quietly discuss the possible responses and come to consensus on the correct response.

4. When I say, "Show Me!" hold up the card that shows the correct answer.

5. You receive one point for each correct response.

Note: Model one question/response round before beginning the game.

Timed Games

Use timed games to help students learn to use their knowledge base quickly to answer questions. Do not allow time to change answers. Make up your own games or use familiar trivia game formats.

Self-Talk

- I know this one; I must mark it and move on!
- I can mark it because I know it is right.
- I won't change it!

BEE BACK

Purpose

- To answer all the questions you know
- To answer easy questions first and quickly
- To prevent you from getting stuck on a problem
- To remember that, if time permits, it pays to return to a question

How To

1. Answer questions you know and move on.

2. If the answer does not come easily or quickly, think to yourself, "I'll be back."

3. Jot down the number of any items you want to check again, if permitted.

4. Complete the test and return to each item you marked.

5. Remember: If time permits, return to the skipped items. Guess, if there is no penalty for guessing.

Applications in the Real World

- Working a jigsaw or other puzzle by completing the easy parts first.
- Learning any new skill, such as driving or playing golf. You start with the easy skills and go back to learn the harder parts.
- Marking an unknown word while reading to look up later.

Early Grades

Signal Time

1. Teach three signals, like these:
   - thumbs up = "I know the answer,"
   - thumbs to the side = "I think I know something about it,"
   - thumbs down = "I don't have a clue about this one."

2. Ask questions on a particular topic and let students answer with the signal that best matches their response.

3. Call on students who give a thumbs-up signal.

4. Discuss the importance of quickly choosing an answer.

Bee Back Attack Song

(Sing to the tune of "Are You Sleeping?")

Bee Back Attack
On the test,
I'll do my best!
I'm a success.
I'm a success.
First I answer the ones I know
To put on a big show.
I'm doing my best,
On this crazy test!

Then go back!
Then go back,

For a bee attack!
For a bee attack!
To those I didn't know,
To give them another go.
I'm doing my best
On this crazy test.

Upper Grades

Color Quest

Give students several multiple choice problems with the following directions:

1. Choose three pens of different colors, such as blue, black, and red.

2. Mark the ones you know in blue.

3. Mark the ones you need to think about with a black dot.

4. Use a red dot to mark the ones you do not know.

5. Answer the problems with the blue dots first.

6. If time allows, answer the problems with a red dot.

Puzzle Play

1. Put a jigsaw puzzle together as the class watches.

2. Place the easy pieces in the puzzle first.

3. Note that it is easier to insert the other pieces once you have the easy ones placed.

4. Point out that this is the way to approach test taking, by completing easy items first. Discuss the value of this strategy.

Bee Back Cheer

Come to an answer that you don't know.
Say, "I'll be back, so on I go!"
Come to an answer that you know.
Say, "Answer, answer, answer those I know."
Mark it and it's time to go!

Try the ones you left again.
You have saved them 'til the end.

Self-Talk

- I'm not going to spend too much time on this one.
- I'll mark this one and be back.
- I must answer the ones I know first.

WHEN IN DOUBT, TRY IT OUT!

Purpose

- To consider each choice as the correct answer
- To eliminate incorrect answers
- To narrow your choices to two possible answers by making educated guesses
- To be sure that you mark one answer when you are in doubt

How To

1. Read the question carefully.

2. Eliminate answers that do not make sense or that you know are wrong.

3. Try out each remaining answer. Does it feel or sound right?

4. For math questions, try the middle option as the correct choice. If it is not the correct answer, you will usually know if you need a larger or smaller number.

5. If you are still unsure, make a smart guess and stick to it.

6. If you have no idea what the answer is, choose an answer at random. This hit-or-miss technique may give you a winner. Find out if there is a penalty for guessing before using this method.

Applications in the Real World

- Guessing who left you a message without leaving a name
- Trying out a bicycle you might buy for size and comfort
- Reminding yourself of a forgotten lock combination or computer password. Try out the possibilities until you hit on the right one.

Early Grades

Chain Links

1. Tell students they are going to practice estimation by guessing how many objects it takes to reach from point A to point B in the school when they are set end to end. For example, how many pencils does it take to reach from the cafeteria to our classroom?

2. Discuss how students reached their answers, emphasizing the value of educated guesses.

Guesstimation Jar

1. Fill a jar with objects such as marbles, pennies, pebbles, or candies.

2. Have students estimate how many items are in the jar.

3. Work through the process of "guesstimation" by asking "How do we know the answer is not _____?" and "How do we know the answer is less than _____?"

4. Count the number of items in the jar aloud. Use squares of paper or index cards and place ten objects on each card. If there are fewer than ten objects on the card, write the number on the card. This is the number left over.

5. Count the number of cards, multiply by ten, add in the number left over, and you have the total.

6. Discuss how well students guessed and why some guesses were closer than others.

Throw It Out Rap

When I throw out wrong answers in my mind
The right answer is easier to find.
When an answer is wrong and I have no doubt
I need to zap it quickly and throw it out!
I strike out the ones that don't fit.
The one that is left is a hit!

Upper Grades

Give It Your Best Shot!

Use sports analogies to emphasize the value of taking a lucky "shot" or guess. Use sports language, such as "slam dunk" from basketball, "over the top" from football, "hole in one" from golf, or "puck luck" from hockey. Lead a discussion and remind students that taking a lucky shot or guess can make someone a winner.

On a Job Hunt

Supply a large number of newspaper classified ad sections. Ask students to do the following activity to teach elimination skills:

1. Pretend you need a job after school.

2. Look in the classified ads for work opportunities.

3. Eliminate the jobs that do not interest you or do not fit your schedule.

4. Make a record of the jobs that suit you.

5. Discuss your selections and elimination process with a partner.

Self-Talk

- Did I complete the easy questions first?
- Can any choices be eliminated?
- Does one answer sound right when I read it?
- Does the answer make sense?

TAKE A DOUBLE TAKE: CHECK, CHECK, CHECK!

Purpose

- To find and correct mistakes
- To realize that if you know the answer but accidentally fill in the wrong circle, you lose points
- To remember to always "check your work"
- To be sure you don't lose points for a simple error

How To

Teach the meaning of "check your work." Model how to check. Students are more likely to check their work when the test is completed early if they do not have other options, such as reading a book or drawing. Students should follow these steps:

1. Quickly look at each answer again, testing it against the question. Is this the answer you meant to mark?

2. See if the number of your response on the answer sheet matches the number of the question on the test form.

3. Look for spaces that are not filled in on your answer sheet. Fill them in with an educated guess.

4. Scan the entire answer sheet for stray marks. Remember that scoring machines may read a stray mark as an answer.

Applications in the Real World

Use the following statements to teach the meaning of the word *check:*

- Looking in the mirror to check your outfit
- Looking again before crossing the street
- Having the car inspected before a long trip

Early Grades

Talk Your Thinking

1. Model your own "processing talk" as you teach learners to complete a problem. For example, as you solve the problem on the board or an overhead, say, "I tried all the answers and have marked the answer in the correct place. I followed the directions." Students are more likely to be aware of and complete these steps when they hear them modeled and practice saying them aloud.

2. Each student finds a partner.

3. Partners each solve a problem, speaking aloud their processing talk as they are modeled by the teacher.

4. After each step, one partner describes the step to the other partner.

5. Students continue to practice checking their work, talking through the process.

Variations: Solving math problems, recipes, science experiments, paper folding.

Upper Grades

Calculator Check

Go over the following special calculator checks with your students:

1. When using a calculator, know how to operate the calculator before the test begins.

2. Remember to clear all functions when each problem is complete.

3. For multistep problems, write the answer to each step on scratch paper.

4. Use extra time to check each step with a calculator.

Journal Activity: Mental Checks

Have students write journal responses to these prompts:

1. Name the steps you use to check a math problem.

2. Write tips that others could use in checking over their work.

3. What do you check before you leave the house each day?

4. What do you check before you leave school each day?

Self-Talk

- Did I think it through again?
- Am I sure it is correct?
- Could I think about it in another way?
- Did I check my answer sheet for stray marks?

SET THE PACE

Purpose

- To develop an awareness of time segments for pacing
- To adjust the speed of your work to the question and subject
- To know when to use fast versus slow reading
- To develop a "feeling" for pacing
- To keep yourself from running out of time

How To

1. When you start a question, quickly decide if it is hard or easy.

2. Speed up for easy questions. Slow down for hard questions.

3. When reading a passage, think about what type of information you are reading: main idea, answer to a particular question, or a detail. Adjust your reading speed to your purpose.

4. Fast pace tips
   - Know the facts, formulas, and terms. Use memory strategies.
   - Know how to read charts, graphs, and time lines.
   - Know when to use a calculator and when to figure the answers in your head.
   - Remember that on some tests, the easiest questions are first.
   - Don't spend too much time on one question; it will "eat up" your time. You will probably know the answer to the next question.
   - Remember: Two minutes is a long time to spend on one question.

Note: Continue to use timers throughout the year so learners have a feeling for various amounts of time.

Applications in the Real World

- Choosing which games you have time to play during recess or before dinner
- Choosing which program, sitcom, or movie you have time to watch before bedtime
- Completing a chore at home within a set of time.

Early Grades

Time Awareness

1. Ask students to make time guesses. For example, ask the following: How long will it take us to walk to the cafeteria? Which is longer, reading class or recess?

2. Use a timer to measure and discuss the length of various activities.

3. Discuss how people keep a sense of time as they do certain tasks.

Pace Race

This activity is designed for competition between the individual student and the clock. Students use poems and stories on various levels of difficulty. Give students the following directions:

1. Read for three minutes.

2. Stop. Count the number of words read.

3. Divide by three or the number of minutes read.

4. Keep a record of your score.

5. Practice on a regular basis to improve the score.

Pacing With the Animals

Instruct students to fill in the blanks and imitate the animal during discussion:

1. When I work through a test, I work like a(n) _____ (animal) because _____.

2. When I don't know the answer and it slows me down, I feel like a(n) _____ (animal) because _____.

3. When I know the answers and move quickly through the test, I feel like a(n) _____ (animal) because _____.

Pace Rap

Challenge students to apply this rap to testing:

Green means go, go, go.

Yellow means slow, slow, slow.

Red means no, no, no.

Upper Grades

Discussion Prompts for Pacing

Ask students to respond to the following prompts:

1. Pacing signals: Red means stop, yellow means caution, and green means go. How do these signals apply to taking a test?

2. Visualize a race car driver or a champion swimmer. Discuss his or her pacing strategies and how to apply the techniques to testing.

3. How is pacing important in my life? How do I feel when I am rushed?

4. How does rushing interfere with test success?

Variation: Illustrate examples of pacing and discuss them.

Color Code the Speed Zones

1. Give each student three small pieces of construction paper in the following colors to match pacing speeds: green is fast, yellow is moderate, and blue is slow.

2. Read aloud short passages of varying difficulty.

3. Have students hold up the color that represents the appropriate reading speed for the material. For example, directions for a math test would be blue, jingles would be green, and a passage from an essay or book would be yellow. Provide time for students to discuss choices with a neighbor or assigned partner.

Self-Talk

- I have used ten minutes. I have __ minutes left to work.
- How much time should I spend on this one?
- Should I read this passage quickly or slowly?
- Did I rush?
- Did I stay within the set time limits?

KEEP ON KEEPING ON

Nothing in the world can take the place of persistence.

—Calvin Coolidge

Purpose

- To get past difficult spots and do your best
- To avoid wasting time
- To learn to apply different approaches or strategies when the first one fails

How To

1. Try educated guesses when the answer is unknown.

2. Read the passage or question for thorough understanding.

3. Try various strategies to answer the question.

4. Keep working until the section is completed.

5. When you feel frustrated or defeated, use a physical activity, such as deep breathing, to relieve the feeling.

Applications in the Real World

- Practicing for perfection in driving, sports, games, crafts, or hobbies
- Trying to solve a difficult problem with a friend or family member

- Applying for a different job after being turned down by a potential employer

Early Grades

Book Share

Share stories and books that teach persistence, such as *The Little Engine That Could* and *The Tortoise and the Hare*.

Piece by Piece

1. Provide activities that are designed to be completed in ongoing stages, such as a complicated structure made of building blocks.

2. Give immediate feedback on stages of success. Include words and phrases related to persistence such as "keep on keeping on."

Upper Grades

Interviews

1. Assign students to interview a successful sports figure, businessperson, or community leader.

2. Tell student to create questions related to the value of persistence such as "How did you become successful?" and "What obstacles have you faced?"

3. Share the results in class.

Persuasive Selling

Give students the following assignment as a writing exercise or role-play:

1. Pretend you are the salesperson who is selling a computer, boat, shoe, piece of jewelry, or car. Your customer is undecided about the purchase. How would you persist in making the sale?

2. Have students role-play the scene.

3. Discuss the persistence strategies used.

4. Discuss how persuasion relates to the "keep on keeping on" skill, or persistence, for test success.

Come On Over to Our Side

1. Divide the class into teams for this cooperative group activity.

2. Use open-ended questions that call for an opinion. Here are some examples:
   - Chocolate is the best ice cream flavor.
   - Red is the most popular color.
   - Baseball is the most popular game.
   - Text messages are the most effective form of communication.

3. Each team comes to consensus on a yes or no answer.

4. Each team brainstorms and lists the reasons for choosing that answer.

5. If teams have opposite opinions, the teams debate, with each team member representative supporting the team's opinion.

6. The team members persist in trying to convince the other teams to agree with their opinion or to "come on over" to their side.

7. At the conclusion of the debate, ask students how persuasion in the activity relates to using persistence in testing.

Self-Talk

- I am going to keep on until I get this right!
- What do I need to do to be able to stick with it?
- What else can I do?
- I will push myself to keep on keeping on.

Attacking 8
Passages and
Solving Problems

When I take a test I feel like my stomach is in my throat. I get but-
terflies in my stomach just like I do before I make a speech. I feel like
my thoughts are moving so fast that I can't slow them down enough
to pull the right pieces together. I know the information is in my
mind somewhere, but my brain just won't squeeze it out. Everything
just seems to vanish when I need it. I talk to myself to calm myself
down and say, "I am not on my way to the electric chair. I know I
studied it."

—Marcia, a college senior

WHY TEACH "ATTACK" SKILLS?

It is easy to be overwhelmed as you begin a test, to feel like there is too
much information to plow through or that your thoughts are buzzing use-
lessly around in your head. These feelings can be prevented, however.
Students who are prepared with ways to approach, or "attack," questions
on tests are less likely to panic and waste time. They pull their thoughts
together and get to work. This way, each learner is able to show what he
or she knows.

An expert test taker internalizes how to attack a passage or problem on
a test. Students need to learn the skills thoroughly and practice them
until they become automatic. Teach these attack strategies with content

information as an intregral and crucial part of lessons. Model the skills, giving learners opportunities to process and explain their thinking as they work. This pondering time lets students make each strategy their own. Also, remember to give students experiences in making personal decisions for selection of the most effective attack strategies.

This chapter provides strategies, activities, tips, and other tricks for teaching thinking, or "attack," skills. Students need to use these skills throughout the year as they tackle a variety of learning tasks. They are crucial for success on test day. By understanding how to approach, or "attack," a question, students become faster and more accurate test takers.

Skills and Strategies Covered in This Chapter

Attack Tactics for Multiple-Choice Questions: Using different approaches to tackle this type of test question

Responding to Open-Ended Test Questions: Writing freely and confidently in response to this type of test question or prompt

Compare and Contrast: Identifying how things are alike and different

Context Clues: Inferring "unknown" information from "known" information in the passage

Cause and Effect: Identifying how or why an event or happening occurred and the result or impact of it

Drawing Conclusions: Creating a summary from facts

Fact Versus Opinion: Distinguishing true or proven statement(s) from an individual's or a group's belief

Zeroing In on the Facts by Scanning: Looking over information quickly to find specific information or details

Getting the Point With Skimming: Looking over or perusing a passage to identify the main idea or overall picture in one's mind

First Things First: Using Sequencing: Focusing on organization, order, and following directions

Teacher's Choice: A hodgepodge of ideas, tips, and strategies

(See also Chapman & King, in press [a].)

ELEMENTS OF THE STRATEGIES IN THIS CHAPTER

We organized each strategy in this chapter to include the following elements. Refer to the previous chapter for a detailed explanation of each element.

- Purpose
- How To
- Applications in the Real World
- Early Grades Activities
- Upper Grades Activities
- Self-Talk

ATTACK TACTICS FOR MULTIPLE-CHOICE QUESTIONS

Purpose

- To have more than one way to approach multiple-choice questions
- To use options for attacking a question
- To discover the strategy that works best in a particular multiple-choice problem

How To

All multiple-choice problems are not approached in the same way. Give students many strategies to attack problems. Here are a few suggestions:

- **Option A:** Study the questions *before* reading a passage or looking at a graph, chart, or map on a test.

  1. Look at the questions to figure out exactly what information is needed before you read.

  2. Find the information.

  3. Check the answer.

- **Option B:** Read the passage and *then* study the questions, so the information is fresh in your mind.

  1. Read the passage, first skimming for the general or main idea, then scan for important supporting information and details.

  2. Answer easy questions first.

  3. Reread harder questions.

- **Option C:** Read the passage, *then* answer the first question. Return to the passage, *then* answer the next question.

1. Skim the passage for the general or main idea.

2. Read the first question and then refer to the passage to find the answer.

3. Use the same procedure with each question or answer choice.

Applications in the Real World

- Following the best directions when there are multiple ways to reach a place
- Troubleshooting or debugging a computer
- Choosing various options or strategies in games or sports

Early Grades

Passage Attack Raps

- Matches Option A above:

  All the questions I read
  Will tell me the information I need.
  Then in the passage I will see
  The correct answer just for me.

- Matches Option B above:

  That new passage I will attack
  To find each and every fact.
  Then the answers I will know
  To all the questions down below.

- Matches Option C above:

  I'll read the passage and try question number one.
  I'll search for the answer. The fun has begun!
  I'll read the passage, then try question number two
  To get my answer from a clue.

Scope It Out!

Show students how to create an imaginary telescope by rolling up a sheet of paper to create a tube. Students look through the "telescope" to "scope out" the answer to a question.

1. Before reading a passage from a text, students read the relevant questions at the end of the section or chapter.

2. Students form partner teams. Partners take turns explaining in their own words what the questions are asking.

3. The teacher reads the passage.

4. When the teacher reads a sentence that answers one of the questions, students show that they have "scoped it out" by holding the telescope up to one eye.

5. At the end of the reading, hold an answer-the-question race.

6. Read a question. Students should rush to put their fingers on the answer in the passage.

7. The partners check each other for accuracy.

8. When partners have an answer, they give an assigned signal, such as standing by their desks or holding up the telescope.

9. Discuss the correct answer before continuing with the other questions.

Eye Spy

Instruct students to do the following:

1. Form partner teams.

2. Read a passage or a favorite story.

3. Individually make up questions about the passage that have short, literal answers.

4. One student asks a question.

5. The partner answers the question and justifies the answer by pointing to the information in the book, saying "Eye Spy!"and reading the answer.

6. Swap roles. Check answers and keep score.

Upper Grades

Detective at Work

Pregame Introduction

1. Select an interesting passage with multiple-choice questions at the end. Place the passage and questions on an overhead.

2. Demonstrate options a, b, and c for attacking the question.

3. Identify the best attack option for each individual question.

4. Leave a list of attack options or strategies on the board or distribute copies of the list.

The Game

1. Introduce a new passage and set of questions.

2. Use a timer. Keep score on the board or on a scorecard.

3. Give the student a point for each correct answer given within the time limit. Ask the student to identify the strategy needed to get the right answer. Give another point for the strategy.

Variation: Ask students to write short autobiographies and develop multiple-choice questions based on their lives. Play the game based on the students' personal stories and questions.

Self-Talk

- Have I tried all strategies?
- Is there another way to do this?
- Which option works for me most of the time?
- I am learning to make quick decisions to choose the right strategy.

RESPONDING TO OPEN-ENDED TEST QUESTIONS

Purpose

- To prepare students for open-ended test statements and questions.
- To remove writing barriers and open minds to the writing process.
- To give students strategies for responding to writing topics and prompts.
- To instill writing confidence in each learner.

How To

How to for Teachers

- Show examples of open-ended test prompts and questions with completed responses.
- Teach students how to read prompts and identify key words.

- Teach brainstorming skills for prewriting with strategies for getting ideas on paper.
- Adapt the following teacher dialogue to teach your students how to generate and record their ideas for the writing responses. Post or display the steps for practice sessions.

The Great Eight: Steps to Writing Responses

1. Pretend you are saying your answer to someone in a conversation.

2. Write the words exactly as you said them in the conversation.

3. Read your response carefully.

4. Add descriptive words and phrases to nouns to help the reader see and understand each one as needed.

5. Add adverbs and phrases to verbs to assist the reader in seeing and understanding the actions.

6. Look for omissions and fill in the incomplete information.

7. Draw a line through mistakes and make corrections.

8. Write your response in paragraph form.

- Students often have trouble responding to open-ended responses and statements. Here are a few barriers that need to be removed:

    Thinking "I can't do this!" Many students have writer's block and think they cannot write. This is a normal reaction to writing in classrooms across grade levels.

    Not knowing enough about the topic. Students cannot write when they do not know anything about the topic. Teach strategies to "read into" the prompt. One way to accomplish this is by continuously digging for meaning and exploring the authors' purposes in all curriculum areas.

    Being unable to stay on the topic. Writers have a tendency to ramble. Teach prewriting skills so students arrange their thoughts around the topic before they begin.

    Being unfamiliar with the terminology. Introduce or review vocabulary words before the writing experience. Practice using context clues to unlock meaning.

    Feeling pressured for time. Begin with short writing assignments to build the writer's confidence. When the writer knows he can write, give longer assignments.

Having feelings of failure. These feelings are often accompanied by expectations of negative consequences. Design writing experiences that provide success for the student. Avoid grading writing assignments when the learner is struggling. Praise, praise, praise! Remember, the writer grows by gradually moving from small steps to giant steps.

Knowing an outsider is going to judge the writing. The student may feel that the "safety net" is gone. Before a major writing test, provide informal writing experiences that are evaluated or graded by students in other classes, another teacher, or a volunteer.

- Provide a variety of writing experiences with different types of writing as outlined in the following chart:

Type of Writing	Purpose	Description
Narrative	*Tells*	<ul><li>Creates a story.</li><li>Presents events around a plot.</li><li>Provides interesting information.</li><li>Often uses dialogue.</li></ul>Examples: story, legend
Descriptive	*Describes*	<ul><li>Paints a picture with words.</li><li>Plays on emotions.</li><li>Uses vivid adjectives, adverbs, and figurative language.</li><li>May contain dialogue.</li></ul>Examples: diary, account
Persuasive	*Convinces*	<ul><li>Uses supporting details to influence.</li><li>Sways the reader to one side of an issue.</li><li>Changes beliefs and attitudes.</li></ul>Examples: ad, editorial
Expository	*Informs*	<ul><li>Provides important details and facts.</li><li>Gives the reader needed information.</li><li>Is clear and concise.</li></ul>Examples: news article, textbook

- Provide students with opportunities to write to a prompt at least once a day throughout the year. When they have daily experiences writing to a prompt, students are more successful using this procedure on the test. Also, remember, the more students write, the better they become with the skill. (See also Chapman & King, in press [b].)

Writing to a prompt can be used at various times with different learning segments. The following list provides suggestions for using writing prompts:

bell-ringing activity	focus activity	journal entry
observations	ticket out the door	survey question
checkpoint	test question	response to content
process	procedure description	reaction to an event
sequence	opinion	fictitious example
factual account	reflection	explanation
prediction	quiz	compare/contrast

How to for Students

- Ask yourself: "What is this saying?"
- Start your prewriting by making a list everything you know.
- Ask yourself this question: "What do I know?"
- Psych yourself up: Say, "I do know _____!"
- Place yourself in the setting or person's shoes.

Applications in the Real World

- Responding to e-mail and text messages
- Answering surveys
- Responding to job application questions

Early Grades

Activity: The Writing Improv

Students need to know how to let their thoughts flow freely to answer open-ended test questions. Practice "writing improv" in game formats and activities. To encourage free writing, do not grade improv activities.

Introduce improv writing by demonstrating the meaning of *improvise* in activities such as the following:

- Ask a musician to demonstrate the improv technique.
- Play or sing a few notes and ask students to sing or hum additional lines.

When students understand the meaning of *improv,* use writing activities such as the following:

- Use intriguing topics or objects and call on volunteers to make up a definition, a description, an explanation, creative uses, or a tall tale.

- Challenge students to write improv responses on small strips of paper, shapes of objects, and sticky notes with content topics throughout the year.

Upper Grades

Activity: Direction Connection

1. Select a place in the room for a Word Resource Board to use for an ongoing activity with direction words found in tests. Add to the display as words related to test directions are encountered.

2. Post direction words that are likely to be on the test as the terms appear in daily assignments and activities. Write them in a variety of fonts, shapes, textures, designs, and bright colors.

3. Form groups and ask students to brainstorm easy ways to remember each definition.

4. Lead the groups to come to consensus on a working definition.

5. Write each definition in a catchy way to match the term.

6. Add difficult or confusing direction words to the Word Resource Board as they are encountered.

Activity: Direction Raps

1. Form cooperative groups of three.

2. Give each group a term found in directions (for example, *brainstorm, predict, persuade, explain, argue, sequence*).

3. Team members brainstorm workable definitions of the term as a recorder makes a list of responses.

4. The team comes to consensus on its favorite and *best* definition.

5. The team creates a rap using the term and definition.

6. A team volunteer writes the term and the composed rap on a poster. If time permits, let the team add an illustration.

7. The teams perform the raps.

8. After each team presents, the term and definition are reviewed through a class discussion. Everyone joins in as the team repeats the rap.

9. The direction rap term posters are displayed for reference during transitions and reviews.

Activity: Word on Words: Test Terms

Select one or two important words or a phrase from the topic of study. Write the selected words vertically in the center of a page. Identify test prompt terms or direction words that fit the puzzle configuration. Write the clues below it.

In the following example "Test Terms" was selected as the key.

Word on Words: Test Terms

1. _ _ _ _ T _ _ _ _
2. _ _ E _ _ _ _ _
3. S _ _ _ _ _ _ _ _ _
4. T _ _ _ _ _

5. _ _ _ T _ _ _ _ _
6. _ _ _ _ E _ _ _ _
7. _ _ _ _ _ _ R _
8. _ _ _ _ M _ _ _
9. _ _ _ S _ _ _ _ _

Clues

1. Name or classify.

2. Tell what you think will happen next.

3. Place the important ideas into a few words.

4. Follow or tell the events in sequence.

5. Find the differences.

6. Place in order.

7. Tell how things or people are alike.

8. Guess.

9. Place in a group or category.

Answer Key

1. identify   2. predict   3. summarize   4. trace   5. contrast

6. sequence   7. compare   8. estimate   9. classify

Variation

Create crossword puzzles and word games using the following terms throughout the year:

analyze	argue	brainstorm	convince	debate	describe
estimate	define	diagram	discuss	estimate	examine
explain	evaluate	interpret	judge	list	name
outline	plot	rank	solve	tell	trace

Adapted from the activity *Word on Words* in Chapman and King, in press (a).

Self-Talk

- Did I identify the direction words in the question or prompt?
- Did I follow the directions?
- Do I need to add anything else to my response to follow the directions completely?

COMPARE AND CONTRAST

Purpose

- To learn the definition of both terms
- To be able to distinguish between the terms
- To identify how things are alike or different
- To use key words to help you read an answer
- To identify the key logical relationship of *same* and *different*

How To

1. Identify key words or phrases that signal a compare or contrast relationship:

similar	different	even though
however	as well as	on the other hand
not only	but also	either

or	although	while
similarly	yet	but
unless		

2. Identify two events, problems, characters, artifacts, or places in the passage, graph, chart, list or question. Have students compare and contrast them. We often ask students to apply the term *compare* and less frequently ask them to *contrast*. Use both of these important terms.

   a. In conversation and assignments, the word *contrast* is not used in isolation but is used with compare and contrast on a Venn diagram. You do not normally hear someone say, "Contrast those two nouns." Use it as a companion to the word *different* across grade levels so learners hear it often and become familiar with the term. For example, ask, "How are these _____ different?" followed by, "Contrast the two _____."

   b. The word *compare* is used across subject areas and throughout life alone or with *contrast*. When the prompt says "compare one object with another," the response may explain how the items are similar and how they are different.

3. If you have trouble comparing or contrasting two objects or ideas and scratch paper is allowed, make a Venn diagram to clarify your thoughts. If there is not enough space in the overlapping section to write how the two objects or persons are alike, write the responses outside of the Venn and draw an arrow from the statement to the overlapping section.

You can also create a graphic organizer for the comparison by drawing a rectangle with two ovals on each side. Write the similarities in the rectangle and the differences in each oval. Refer to the section "Graphic Organizers: An Overview" in Chapter 4 for more information on using Venn diagrams and variations of the organizer.

Applications in the Real World

- Compare entertainment options such as sports events, movies, television shows, and video games.
- Compare yourself to a friend, brother, sister, parent, celebrity or person you are studying.
- Compare and contrast vacation spots to select the best destination.
- Decide how one item, such as a pair of shoes, a computer, a cell phone, or a game, is better than another item.

Early Grades

Be a Spy: Compare and Contrast Rap

Be a spy
Give it a try
Alike or different
What am I?
Look at me closely
And you will see
Many differences
In you and me.
Find the ways we are different or the same
Be a spy and play our game.

Just Like Me

1. Assign partners. One student is named A. The second student is named B.

2. Have students face each other.

3. Student A makes statements that can be answered with the statement "Just like me." For example, Student A says, "I live in a house," and Student B replies, "Just like me."

4. After five statements, students change roles.

5. Points may be awarded to teams for the number of "Just like me" responses.

Note: Statements that are not answered "Just like me" are contrasts. For example, if Student B has a dog and the other does not, this is in contrast or difference.

Upper Grades

Create a Venn Diagram

1. Ask students to compare and contrast the weather in two consecutive months.

2. Plot weather information on a line graph daily for two months and use the data to create a Venn diagram.

3. Select other sample topics to use in Venn diagram activities that are relevant to the students' content topics or interests. Some of their interests include books, songs, movies, games, television shows, special events, and clothes.

Connection Blasts

1. Name two items that are not usually associated with each other such as television and book, chair and radio, notebook and train, boots and paper bag, bicycle and rug. Select two objects from the unit of study for review of content information.

2. Assign three minutes for partners to brainstorm the ways the items are alike. You will be amazed how innovative their answers are!

The Old Meets New

1. Ask students to brainstorm old and new pairs, such as new and antique items, modern and ancient homes, old and new vehicles, and songs from their own generation versus their parents' generation.

2. As a class or individually, create drawings to illustrate the contrasts.

Metaphor Mania

1. Use metaphors to illustrate the compare-and-contrast strategy.

2. Model the process using this prompt: This _____ (subject or topic) is like _____ because they both _____.

3. Instruct students to invent and share their own metaphors for a chosen subject or topic.

4. Discuss how the subject is different from its partner in the metaphor.

Self-Talk

- How are these alike?
- How are they different?
- How does _____compare to _____ ?

- Should I create a Venn diagram to assist my thinking?
- What is the meaning of *compare?*
- What is the meaning of *contrast?*

CONTEXT CLUES

Purpose

- To be able to answer a question even if you do not know all the words in the question or passage. Context clues help you discover the meaning of a word so it does not interfere with your comprehension.
- To use words in a sentence or passage to help you discover the meaning of an unknown word or phrase
- To figure out the meaning of a word, phrase, or sentence by plugging in information you already know

How To

1. Look around in the sentence or passage for clues when you come across a word or phrase you do not know.

   a. Look at the words before the unknown word. What are they telling you?

   b. Look at the words after the unknown word. What are they telling you?

2. Use all of the known words in the passage to help you. Look for definitions, antonyms, synonyms, comparisons, examples, meanings, contrasts, and descriptive words as clues. All readers need to know how to apply these skills automatically.

3. Try this sentence sample: "The sunset had shades of crimson and indigo that reminded us of red flowers and deep blue water." If the words *crimson* and *indigo* are unknown, the description of the flowers as *red* and water as *blue* unlock the meanings.

4. Plug in, or substitute, a known word or phrase for an unknown word or phrase. For example, imagine that you read, "The football player was exhilarated when the ball passed over the goalposts." If you don't know the meaning of the word *exhilarated,* substitute a guess, such as *happy, excited, or joyful,* to unlock the meaning of the sentence based on the context.

If–Then

Ask students to fill in the blanks with information from their own lives. Each statement has a cause and effect. Teach that *cause* and *effect* are two terms to be aware of while reading, writing, and engaging in conversation.

If I turn here, then I will _____.

If I go to _____ with my friends, then it will _____.

If I say, _____, then they will feel _____.

If I go to _____ , then my parents will _____.

If I _____ , then I will _____ .

Upper Grades

Domino Effect

Demonstrate the classic domino effect.

1. Stand at least 20 dominoes approximately 1/4 inch apart.
2. Ask students to predict what will happen when the first domino is pushed into the second domino.
3. Demonstrate by pushing the first domino.
4. Discuss the cause and effect of each action in this process.

Variations: Roll a marble into the first domino or blow it over. Have students brainstorm creative ways to "cause" the dominoes to fall over and describe the "effect."

Match Game

Invent match games like the one in Figure 8.3 from the content information. Draw the causes and effects from material you have been studying. Have the students make up their own match games to share with peers as a review before a teacher-made test.

FIGURE 8.3

Match Game

Cause	Effect
poor nutrition	drowsiness
no sleep	exhaustion
a nail in a tire	cavities
failure to study for a test	flat tire
swimming too long	a low grade

The Event From Both Sides

In this activity, students role-play cause and effect interactions.

1. Students divide into teams of three or four.

2. Assign each team a cause and effect scene or instruct teams to brainstorm their own ideas.

3. Ask teams to create role-plays to dramatize cause and effect.

4. Each team prepares and performs the cause and effect scene.

5. The other students guess the cause and effect being portrayed.

Possible role-plays include the following: drug pusher with students who want to stay drug-free, a key and a lock, cars in a collision, characters from a story or from history in a problem-solving situation, characters stranded on a desert island, and a virus encountering the immune system.

Cause and Effect Poem

The reason "Why" is the cause, you see.
It's the reason it happened to you and me.
The result of what happened is the effect on it.
Examine it closely as you look at it bit by bit.
An effect does not happen without a cause, you know.
First comes the cause. Then effects come fast or slow.

Self-Talk

- The cause occurs before the effect ("c" before "e").
- If this occurs, it will be a cause, and what will happen is the effect.
- What caused this event to happen?
- What are the effects of this happening?

DRAWING CONCLUSIONS

Purpose

- To know how to pull important information together
- To know and use facts or other information to reach an answer
- To know how to infer, or fill in, missing pieces of information

How To

1. Read the test item or passage carefully.

2. Note important facts and information.

3. Decide if there are any important missing pieces. Use everything you know to find the answer to what you don't know.

4. Pull all of your thoughts together.

5. Using the information you have, draw the best conclusion about what the writer means.

Applications in the Real World

- Listening to all sides of an issue before drawing a conclusion
- Finding a solution to a problem in life based on all the information
- Making a decision after looking at all options and drawing a conclusion

Early Grades

Footprint Hunt

1. Present pictures of various animal footprints.

2. Brainstorm information about the animal that can be inferred from the print. Is it big or small? Is it catlike, doglike, or birdlike? How many toes does it have? Where does it live? Search for other interesting facts.

3. Ask students to conclude, based on information, which animal made the footprint.

Target Practice

1. On the board or on a large piece of paper, create a grid like the one in the upper portion of Figure 8.4.

2. Give each student a sheet of paper. Tell them to create their own versions of the grid like the one in the lower portion of Figure 8.4.

3. Form A/B partners. Partner A places a secret mark on his or her grid. Partner B guesses where the mark is by calling out intersecting points.

4. Students take turns trying to hit the target.

5. Discuss how the students hit the target by drawing conclusions.

FIGURE 8.4

	1	2	3	4	5	6	7	8
A								
B								
C								
D								
E								

	1	2	3	4	5	6	7	8
A								
B								
C								
D								
E								

Upper Grades

Mystery Scenes

1. Place students in small groups.

2. Each group invents a short scene that contains a mystery.

3. Act out the scene. The student audience lists the hints or clues they find to solve the mystery.

4. Form partners to share the clues or solutions to the mystery.

Arrow Organizer

Model how to use an arrow to organize the process of drawing a conclusion.

1. Draw a wide arrow on the board. Label the long arrow shaft with the topic under discussion. Pick a topic to use as an example as you model the process. For example, the topic might be an unknown word in a story, such as *dinero.*

2. Draw slanted lines coming out of the arrow like the feathers. The slanted lines are reserved for known facts about the topic. Facts might include the following: the character who uses the word is

from Mexico, many Spanish words end in *o,* and the conversation in the scene is about money.

3. Write your conclusion at the arrow's point: *dinero* is the Spanish word for "money."

Self-Talk

- What does this tell me?
- I gather all ideas to reach a conclusion.
- Let me read this and find the meaning.
- I conclude that _____.

FACT VERSUS OPINION

Purpose

- To find what is true or factual
- To find out someone's belief or opinion
- To be able to distinguish between the two terms

How To

1. Ask yourself: Can this be proved? Is this true? Is there evidence to support this statement? If the answer to these questions is yes, it is a fact.

2. Ask yourself: Is this something a person thinks or believes to be true? If the answer to this question is yes, it is an opinion.

Applications in the Real World

- Choosing which candidate to trust more in an election
- Deciding which skateboard model to buy after comparing what friends, advertisers, and consumer reporters say about it
- Reaching a verdict in a jury trial
- Analyzing strong, persuasive voices and advertisements

Early Grades

Spider Organizer

See Figure 4.2 for information on how to use a spider organizer to separate fact from opinion.

Fact and Opinion Rap

Facts are true things you are learning as you go.
Facts are the knowledge and trivia you know.
Opinions are points of view
That impact the way you think, play, and do.
Facts are in the news and a history book.
Your opinion is a belief or the side you took.

Pet Facts and Opinions

1. Instruct students to observe a class pet.

2. Each student gathers data on the pet's actions.

3. Students write factual statements to describe the actions, such as "The gerbil ran on its wheel for three minutes." Label the statements with an *F* (fact).

4. Students write opinion statements to describe the actions, such as "It ran because it needed exercise." Label the statements with an *O* (opinion).

5. Share the results and check that all fact statements are accurate and all opinion statements are beliefs or personal ideas.

Best of the Best

1. Instruct students to brainstorm reasons why their class is the best.

2. Challenge students to use a specific number of facts and opinions.

3. Label each response as fact or opinion.

Upper Grades

Choices From Many Voices Poem

Opinions I can have, you see
My guesses and feelings are free.
But you do not have to agree
With what I may believe you see
My opinions are what I think should be
And they come from inside me.
I find opinions in polls and ads

Editorials, on television, and in funny fads.
But I will always make my choices
After I hear facts and opinions from many voices.

In the Game

1. Bring in a video or audiotape of a sports announcer calling a game.

2. Ask students to make a two-column chart to separate facts and opinions.

3. Have students listen carefully to the tape once or twice.

4. Students list facts they hear in the left column and opinions in the right column.

5. Call on several students to share their findings.

6. Discuss the impact of the announcer's words in swaying the audience.

Variation: Have students read an editorial page in a local newspaper, make a chart to separate facts and opinions, and debate the results.

Headliners With Fact and Opinion

Instruct students to create a list of facts and opinions about a famous person. Categories of famous people could include rock stars, sports figures, authors, politicians, explorers, actors, inventors, scientists, or historical figures. Use figures from subjects studied in class.

Self-Talk

- What does this person, author, or character believe?
- Can that be proved?
- Did that really happen?
- I understand what others think. Now, what do I think?

ZEROING IN ON THE FACTS BY SCANNING

Purpose

- To find important details that support the main idea in a passage
- To find pieces of information that answer these questions: Who? What? Where? When? Why? How? How much? How many?

- To be able to "put my finger on" the needed information quickly
- To be able to eliminate unimportant information quickly

How To

1. Decide exactly what piece of information you need.

2. Search for the information by looking for a key word or phrase.

3. Pass your eyes quickly over the entire passage until the key word or phrase "jumps out."

4. Focus on the sentence or sentences around the key word or phrase and ignore the rest of the passage.

5. Extract the information you need.

6. Consider the following fact-finding clues when you read a passage:
   - *When* and *where* are usually found near the beginning.
   - Problems are usually found in the middle.
   - Solutions are usually found toward the end.

Applications in the Real World

- Supporting your opinion with important facts
- Sorting through lots of information on the Internet to find specific data
- Finding the time of a movie or television program in a schedule
- Looking for the score of a game in the sports section

Early Grades

Facts in the Spotlight

1. Write a passage on the board or on a large piece of paper.

2. Place the text so it is visible to everyone.

3. Dim the lights. Use a penlight to spot key words, phrases, numbers, or sentences as you read them aloud.

Facts in the Scene

1. Ask a group of students to role-play an important part of a story or event from a reading passage.

2. Tell them they can use only the facts in the written passage to establish who, what, where, when, and how this event or story happened.

3. Discuss where in the passage they found the information they used in the role-play activity.

Upper Grades

Fact-Finding Rap

I'll learn the facts I need to know
The information is needed to grow.
The Internet, books, and the news
Are some sources for facts I can use.
I can keep them in my mental file
And on tests be ahead by a mile.

The Eyewitness

Introduce this activity by telling students that the ability to identify details and facts is extremely important to eyewitnesses of automobile accidents and robberies.

1. Choose one student to stand in front of the class.

2. Instruct the class to look closely at the chosen student.

3. Ask the student to leave the classroom and change three things about his or her appearance.

4. Bring the student back in front of the class.

5. Tell students to check their attention to details by identifying the three changes.

Scanning Scavenger Hunts

Here are some scavenger hunt ideas that teach students how to scan for information:

1. Look for specific information in a newspaper or magazine article.

2. Find words in an index.

3. Find words or numbers in a text.

4. Find a name in a game roster.

You may use a timer or give points to the student who first finds the identified information.

Self-Talk

- What is the important fact?
- The answer is here in front of me!
- I can quickly look through the unimportant information.
- I'm going to scan it to find just the facts I need.

GETTING THE POINT WITH SKIMMING

Purpose

- To separate details from the main idea
- To understand the most important thought in a passage
- To identify the reason the passage was written
- To avoid being distracted by unimportant details

How To

1. Look over the passage quickly to find the main idea or general thoughts. Skim for no more than 20 seconds to get a rough idea of what the section is about. Don't stop to study detail in any part that you don't understand.

2. Use your fingers or an index card as an eye guide, as needed. Ignore unimportant words, such as *the, a, an, but, this,* and *that.*

3. Concentrate on the passage's opening and closing.

4. Remember that the main idea in a long passage is *usually* in the first three sentences.

5. The main point of a paragraph is often in the first or last sentence.

6. Read all headings, explanations in bold and italics, as well as all graphics.

7. Try the following ways to tackle a passage on a test using skimming:

   - **Option A:** Read the passage carefully from start to finish. Don't try to remember details because you won't need to remember irrelevant information.
   - **Option B:** Skim to get the general idea, or "catch the drift," of the passage and go directly to the questions. Refer to the passage as you answer each question.
   - **Option C:** Skim to get general meaning then return to read more thoroughly. Two readings are better than one. Proceed with the questions.

Applications in the Real World

- Telling a friend about a movie, book, or event, starting with the most important idea and then filling in details
- Looking over a newspaper article to find the main idea quickly
- Previewing a library book before you choose it

Early Grades

Table the Main Idea

1. Using a picture of a table or a real table, write or place something representing the main idea on the table.

2. Write or place objects representing details on the table legs or under the table.

Supporting Columns

1. Draw a picture of a roof and write out a main idea on the roof.

2. Draw columns underneath and place a supporting detail on each one.

Take a Peek

Instruct students to do the following:

1. Preview all pictures and graphics in a unit or book before reading.

2. Tell a partner what the unit or book is about from the information gathered in the "Take a Peek" preview.

Upper Grades

In the Headlines

1. Cut headlines from several articles in newspapers.

2. Students skim the articles for details and match the headlines.

Highlight Delight

1. Students read a passage individually, highlighting important ideas.

2. Students form partner groups to compare highlights.

3. If partners do not agree on the importance of a highlight, each one defends the choice until they reach agreement.

4. Partners make a list of key highlighted ideas.

5. Partners create one to three sentences representing the most important ideas and facts in the assigned passage.

6. Lead a discussion of how this activity shows why skimming is important.

Skim Game

1. Identify paragraphs for students to use in the skim game.

2. Form student pairs, Students A and B.

3. Give students less than half the time it should take for them to read the passage.

4. Student A tells B all remembered facts while Student B jots down the recalled facts without worrying about correct spelling. Student B writes everything recalled by Student A without adding to the facts.

5. Students A and B find the answers in the passage and place check marks or tiny sticky tabs by correct responses as they find each one.

6. The team receives a point for each correct fact found while skimming.

7. Student B takes a turn while player A writes.

Self-Talk

- I can skim or scan the passage to find the answer.
- In one sentence, this is about. . . .
- I can identify the main idea and give supporting details.
- What is this paragraph telling me?
- What is the author's point or purpose?
- I get the point!

FIRST THINGS FIRST: USING SEQUENCING

Purpose

- To learn to place events or things in order
- To understand when events occurred during a period
- To learn how to follow directions or steps in order

How To

1. Identify key words or phrases that indicate sequence:

meanwhile	not long after	finally
before	between	first
tomorrow	on (date)	second
then	beginning	last
today	middle	now
after	end	

2. Use a time line to mark and remember the periods of time.

3. Number events of a passage, a story, or a procedure in sequential order to identify what happens first, second, third, and so forth.

4. Visualize the events in a sequence.

Applications in the Real World

- Before inviting a friend over to your house, organize your to-do list to make this happen: (1) determine whom to invite, (2) decide the purpose of the visit, (3) ask permission, (4) set day and time, and (5) call the friend.
- Identify sequential tasks in planning a party. Example: (a) Identify the type of party or celebration it will be. (b) Decide where you want to hold the event. (c) Identify contacts for permission and support. (d) What will you do to prepare for the party? (e) What do you need to buy? (f) Who will be invited? (g) What food will be served? (h) How will you invite them? (i) How will they RSVP?
- Complete routine tasks in sequential order, such as getting ready for bed each night, for example (1) taking a bath, (2) putting on your pajamas, (3) brushing your teeth, (4) reading a book, and (5) turning out the light.

Early Grades

Tape Talk

1. Use a roll of cash register tape or long, narrow strips of paper.

2. Write three words on the tape to begin a story. Sample beginning: "A boy was. . . ."

3. Let each student add three words to the story and pass the tape to the next classmate.

4. Read the story aloud. Mark and discuss the "sequencing" words in the story, such as *then, next, first,* and *finally.* If they are not in the story, add the words to make the story flow.

Action Scenes

1. Students act out the scenes in a play or story.

2. Discuss each action in the scene using sequencing terms.

3. Ask students to draw the sequence of actions illustrating what happened first, second, etc.

Sequence of Events for Test Day

1. Students make a to-do list for a successful test morning.

2. Each item is checked as it is accomplished.

Example: Give students a list to sequence. Students place items on the list in sequence:

_____ Eat a good breakfast.

_____ Check your supplies.

_____ Get to school early.

_____ Dress in comfortable clothes.

Story Lines

1. Place four chairs side by side in a row.

2. Above each chair, place a sign that reads as follows:

    Chair #1: "First, I _____."

    Chair #2: "Next, I _____."

    Chair #3: "Then, I _____."

    Chair #4: "In the end, I _____."

3. Have a student sit in each chair.

4. The student in chair #1 begins the story using the prompt written on the sign above that chair.

5. The students in chairs #2 and #3 add to the story.

6. The student in chair #4 ends the story.

7. If time permits, four more students sit in the chairs and tell a new story with their story lines.

Upper Grades

The Times of My Life

1. Each student makes a time line beginning with birth to his or her present age.

2. Special events are indicated on the time line. Examples: "I started crawling. I started walking. I got a dog. I started to school. My little sister was born. I went to_____."

Mimes in the Scene

1. Divide the class into five groups.

2. Read a book with specific events.

3. Assign a scene to each group to create a freeze-frame dramatization.

4. Groups place themselves in order according to the sequence of events.

5. Groups freeze as mimes in the scene.

Step by Step

Instruct students to try the following:

1. Read specific directions to play a game or learn a new hobby.

2. Divide a sheet of paper into six equal sections and number each section.

3. Draw one step for the new game or hobby in each numbered section.

4. Share the drawing to see if the directions are clear.

Self-Talk

- Did I use the sequence clue words to find the answer?
- Did I plot the events in order?
- I'll check my answer by visualizing a time line.
- What happened at the beginning? In the middle? At the end?

TEACHER'S CHOICE

Purpose and How To

The following suggestions and ideas were compiled to assist in preparing students for tests. Use this collection of effective strategies and tips as needed.

Multiple-Choice Cues for Success

Take the High Road: A Jingle

If I take the time to go through this process,
I will be on the high road to test success.

Multiple-Choice Strategy Collection

Provide students with these strategies; each one can be used with all multiple-choice tests. Strategically use each one in your plans.

1. Try each answer with the stem, prompt, or question.

2. Read all answer choices.

3. Listen to your own thinking about the answer.

4. Eliminate the answers you know are wrong.

5. Guess if there is no penalty for guessing.

6. Think like the test maker, who may be trying to trick you.

7. When in doubt, go for the long answer. Long answers are used more often than short answers.

8. When there are two opposite answers, choose one of them.

9. If you don't have a clue about the correct answer, choose the middle one. Test makers like to place correct answers between other choices.

10. Look carefully at each incorrect answer when the practice test is reviewed. Write the correct answer on your paper.

11. Analyze your response. Ask yourself why you did not find the correct answer. Was it carelessness? Did you study? Did you forget the answer?

12. Keep an intermission log. After each test, jot down your thoughts about the testing experience. Decide what action you need to take between tests to improve your test-taking performance. Include your successes and the areas you need to improve. Make a list of the strategies that work best for you. End the journal entry with a statement to celebrate the completion of your hard work, such as, "I gave my best on the test!"

Placing Change 9
in the Spotlight

PULLING IT ALL TOGETHER

Many aspects of standardized testing are out of our control, but they are here to stay. We must identify the aspects of the tests that are in our control, such as the preparation of students for tests and the use of the test results. We can take the test scores and examine areas of strength and weakness that need to be addressed as an entire state and by district, school, class, and individual student. This provides data that can be used in a productive way for improvement. For instance, if a school interprets data that identify weak areas, the staff needs to plan strategically the role of each member to target the students' areas of weakness across subject areas so they become areas of strength. A classroom teacher examines class or individual scores to target individual needs strategically so each student learns the skill, concept, process, or standard. (See also Chapman & King, 2005.)

Students often ask, "Why do I have to take this test?" especially when they are forced to endure grueling rounds of seemingly meaningless tests. They can be forgiven for asking the question, especially if the adults around them convey only anxiety or indifference about the process. Instead of this attitude, learners need to view tests as one more way to show what they know. This can be emphasized during daily classroom assessments by referring to the learning that is taking place. Also, explain that the class is a team and that each individual test score becomes a part of the class score, similar to the way a football player's points contribute to the team's score.

As educators, you, too, can ask probing questions about testing. Be a catalyst for change at your school. Spark a conversation among teachers, administrators, parents, community members, and students in a spirit of congenial inquiry Conversations lead to action through step-by-step planning to improve test performance.

All students and educators will benefit from standardized testing when we move away from dreading the event and plan it as a celebration of learning.

Change Happens With the Right Focus

Do higher scores on tests mean that students are learning more today than in previous years? Students are learning more today, but that is not necessarily the reason some states' test scores are improving. Nonetheless, many federal government and state officials believe if a student can pass the state exams, educators and students are doing a better job.

Some states are lowering passing scores, replacing some difficult questions with simpler ones, and/or assigning more weight to easier questions, so more students pass the mandated tests. Aren't they missing the point? We need to design tests so students can show what they know or what they have learned. The results need to be used to guide the learners to success in their academic activities and in their daily lives.

We believe standardized tests are here to stay. The changes made to them are out of your control. However, you need to use everything in your control to make changes to improve test results and learning.

To create change with the right focus for each learner's success on tests, all educators need to make a strong commitment to each of the following items:

- Teach the skills and content materials so students retain the information for tests and future learning experiences.
- Give students opportunities to use the information they have learned and internalized in reviews with stimulating activities and challenging events. Link the previously learned information to new content, strategies, and skills.
- Strategically plan differentiated assignments and activities to meet the unique needs of each learner.
- Demonstrate that you know all students can learn in each instructional segment and practice session. Remember you have an entire school year to make a difference. Never give up on a student.
- Teach test-taking strategies in all content areas throughout the year, instilling positive attitudes toward testing
- Prepare students mentally, emotionally, and physically, using the ideas in this book as a springboard to make each testing scene a celebration of learning.

Change Happens With the Right People

Change happens when the right people believe there is a need to do things differently. A dedicated group of individuals can make a big difference in the attitudes students have toward testing and learning. Students, parents, teachers, administrators, and staff members need to work as a bonded team to improve test success and lifelong learning.

Administrator's Change Checklist

All During the Year

☐ 1. Analyze and study the current testing scene, looking closely at the school's data to identify the strengths and needs with your own personal view.

☐ 2. Form staff teams to interpret results by examining areas of strength and weakness.

☐ 3. Establish time for interpreting test results.

☐ 4. Identify and celebrate strengths with all stakeholders.

☐ 5. Prioritize the weaknesses for implementing change.

☐ 6. Share brain research related to optimal learning.

☐ 7. Encourage positive approaches and be a supporter while communicating with students, staff, and parents.

☐ 8. Let everyone know by your words and actions that teachers are teaching and students are learning.

For Test Week

☐ 1. Define participant roles.

☐ 2. Provide test guidelines and security.

☐ 3. Notify parents of their roles during the testing event.

☐ 4. Adjust schedules and remove all interruptions to provide a quiet testing environment.

☐ 5. Schedule events to create hype for test success.

☐ 6. Send encouraging supportive announcements to teachers and students.

☐ 7. Include classes and other opportunities for physical activity before and between tests.

Teacher's and Support Staff's Change Checklist

All During the Year

☐ 1. Analyze the latest testing data.

☐ 2. Implement a plan to continue to engage areas of strength and improve the weak areas.

☐ 3. Teach the necessary content information, skills, and concepts that students need.

☐ 4. Motivate, and praise success.

☐ 5. Teach students to be self-regulated learners.

☐ 6. Infuse test-taking strategies in content activities and informal tests.

☐ 7. Prepare students for changes that will occur during the formal testing environment.

For Test Week

☐ 1. Create an environment that is normal and routine.

☐ 2. Be a confidence builder by letting students know that they are ready for the tests.

☐ 3. Become familiar with the test format and directions.

☐ 4. Prepare the proctor and other volunteers in the room.

☐ 5. Strategically plan physical activities or active stretch breaks during transitions.

☐ 6. Have materials available and organized.

Parents' Change Checklist

All During the Year

☐ 1. Create and maintain positive learning experiences.

☐ 2. Set high expectations for your child.

☐ 3. Know he or she is capable and express it.

☐ 4. Learn as much as you can about the test for your child.

☐ 5. Talk to your child in positive ways about testing.

☐ 6. Keep the line of communication open with the teacher to express your concerns and questions about your child's personal or academic needs.

For Test Week

☐ 1. Listen to your child's feelings about taking tests. Do not dwell on their negative comments.

☐ 2. Prepare your child mentally, emotionally, and physically.

☐ 3. Show love and support and let your child know you expect the BEST!

Change Happens With the Right Resources

If appropriate resources, such as the right people, equipment, materials, and technology, are available, the plan will work. Before seeking outside assistance, brainstorm to identify all available resources to implement the plan.

Be cautious about purchasing materials and resources that promote a quick fix for raising test scores. The content and skills must transfer to daily learning experiences. Keep in mind that *all* test preparations can be designed to support and enhance each student's love of learning.

Change Happens With the Right Attitude

A positive, optimistic team with an established knowledge base and the right attitude will work as the catalyst for effective change. When people have the opportunity to work in ways that make them comfortable, they will accomplish more, so encourage all participants to select responsibilities that bring their talents center stage. Recognize and celebrate each successful step toward change. The Successful Team Inventory (Figure 9.1) is designed as a springboard for needed conversations about fostering the right attitude.

Change Happens With the Right Plan

When test scores come in, use the data for change and not to reinforce defeatism. Do not tolerate statements such as "There's nothing we can do; the scores don't mean anything anyway." Another negative response may

FIGURE 9.1

Successful Team Inventory

Instructions: Read each statement and circle a number to indicate how your team works. Use the results to begin a discussion about changes needed to create or maintain an optimal test scene.

		Disagree		Agree	
1.	We have a clear vision of what we want to accomplish.	1	2	3	4
2.	We have established and discussed our roles.	1	2	3	4
3.	We use each member's talents and areas of expertise.	1	2	3	4
4.	We respectfully listen to all ideas.	1	2	3	4
5.	We continuously analyze data to make improvements for learners.	1	2	3	4
6.	We continue to strengthen our strengths.	1	2	3	4
7.	We analyze weak areas for improvement.	1	2	3	4
8.	We teach test-taking strategies as an integral part of our everyday curriculum.	1	2	3	4
9.	We take pride in knowing the unique and diverse needs of each learner.	1	2	3	4
10.	We develop self-directed learners who can readily apply information and skills they have learned.	1	2	3	4
11.	Our team seeks information and opinions to improve teaching and learning for test success.	1	2	3	4
12.	We have reasonably balanced participation in conversation.	1	2	3	4
13.	We share responsibilities equally.	1	2	3	4
14.	Outsiders would say that we work well together.	1	2	3	4
15.	Humor and laughter are a regular part of our work atmosphere.	1	2	3	4
16.	The climate is relaxed and open.	1	2	3	4
17.	We exemplify the belief that we are Great and Getting Greater.	1	2	3	4

Comments:

_____

_____

_____

_____

_____

be complacency. You may hear "We're doing pretty well here compared to other schools, do why so we need to change?"

Do not ignore test scores. They provide crucial information about your students' knowledge, test-taking skills, and comfort levels. They highlight strengths and weaknesses in the curriculum and can be used to identify effective and ineffective instructional strategies. In the following section, we provide a planning process to help you initiate procedures to move from test results to an improvement plan.

Stepping Into Change: A Planning Process

Adapt the following steps to develop a team plan for improving the testing scene:

1. Gather and interpret the most recent testing data.
   - Identify strengths and weaknesses.
   - Describe improvements needed and prioritize.

2. Analyze the testing environment.
   - Identify strengths and weaknesses.
   - List and prioritize improvements needed.

3. Choose the top three items from the prioritized improvements lists.

4. Seek volunteers and assign specific responsibilities to team members.

5. Provide a time line with scheduled meetings and progress reports.

6. Monitor needs and celebrate improvements throughout the process.

THE PARENT'S ROLE IN THE TEST SCENE

Parents are the key.

—Sonya Bailey

Parents naturally have an innate concern for their child's failures and successes. Use their input as a valuable source to help you understand the needs of each member of your class. Maintain open lines of communication between you and the parents to foster a positive learning and testing environment.

In today's society, students may not live with a biological parent. Be cognizant of the family structure so you can appropriately communicate with those responsible for the student's well-being.

Gathering Information From Parents

Communicating with parents about the learner's social, emotional, and academic needs is vital. Survey parents throughout the year. Use the sample survey in Figure 9.2 to identify their child's reactions to testing and learning. Use the information from the survey to assist you in understanding the student.

Helping Parents Understand the Testing Scene

As coaches, prompters, and fans of their children, parents want to be able to support their child's daily learning activities and performance on tests. Keep parents informed about testing and the analyzed results. Be prepared and open to any related questions and concerns.

Keep in mind that individuals who are not in the field of education may not understand the terminology associated with tests. See Figure 5.4 for more information on the meaning of terms associated with testing.

Inquiring parents want to know . . .

Before the Test

- What is a standardized test?
- What does it measure?
- How do I know what the percentile score means?
- How does the teacher use the test results?
- How will the school use the results?
- What can we do at home to prepare for the test?

After the Test

- What do the scores mean?
- How did my child's scores compare to other students' scores?
- What were my child's strongest areas?
- What areas of need were found?
- How will my child's educational program be changed?
- How can I use the results to help my child?

Communicating Test Success Strategies to Parents

The sample letter, information, and handouts presented here are designed to help you give parents suggestions to develop positive approaches to tests. Parents are usually the students' most influential

FIGURE 9.2

Understanding My Child's Reaction to Tests: A Survey

Instructions: Read each statement and circle yes or no.

Child's Name _____

My child . . .

1.	likes to take tests.	Yes	No
2.	forgets to study for tests.	Yes	No
3.	talks to me about each test.	Yes	No
4.	asks for assistance when studying for tests.	Yes	No
5.	shows a strong interest in preparing for tests.	Yes	No
6.	and I have a battle over studying for tests.	Yes	No
7.	complains about tests.	Yes	No
8.	likes to study for tests with a friend.	Yes	No
9.	knows how to study effectively for tests.	Yes	No
10.	studies for tests with little or no assistance.	Yes	No
11.	studies for tests at the last minute.	Yes	No
12.	is more concerned about getting good grades than learning the information.	Yes	No
13.	knows the purpose of tests.	Yes	No
14.	has a positive attitude toward testing.	Yes	No

Comments:

_____

_____

_____

_____

_____

Parent's Signature _____ Date _____

teachers. The amount of parent involvement usually predicts the student's attitude and drive to excel on tests.

Parents need to know the wonderful experiences their child is having at school! Often, the only time parents are contacted by the school is when their child is in trouble. Contact parents and praise them for the job they are doing with their child at home. Tell parents to convey their beliefs and confidence to the student and express their high expectations.

When parents are involved, students achieve more regardless of socioeconomic status, cultural background, or parents' educational level. Learners exhibit more positive attitudes and behavior with routine communication between the home and school. Teachers, students, and parents benefit when they work together for the learner's best interest.

Use various lines of communication to inform parents about the value of positive approaches to tests. Phone calls, message boards, Web sites, bulletin boards, newsletters, open house presentations, room meetings, and other communication tools can be used to share positive ways to develop test-wise students.

Sample Parent Letter

The sample letter in Figure 9.3 is designed to inform parents about their role in making the test a positive experience. Adapt the letter to your own situation. You may want to include the other information in this section, such as Figure 9.4, Test Talk, and Figure 9.5, Tips for Parents, as handouts to accompany the letter. All of these resources can be adapted for use during parent-teacher conferences and meetings.

Testing Conversations at Home

Parents' comments about tests greatly influence the child's attitudes and general self-confidence. As parents discuss the scores with other parents, friends, and relatives and the child, their anxiety becomes contagious.

On test day, teachers hear students repeating parents' test reminders, such as, "Mom said I'd better pass the test or I would be in trouble." Many times, these words are repeated in whispers, but they have obviously been instilled deeply in the student. It is important that parents and teachers avoid comments that create test anxiety.

On the other hand, parents need to communicate a genuine feeling of pride in knowing that their child has learned an immense amount of information and will have the opportunity to show what he or she knows on the test.

FIGURE 9.3

Sample Parent Letter

Dear _____ (parent),

Your child will be taking the annual achievement test later this year. To prepare him/her for this event, I have compiled some information for you. The suggestions are made to help your child feel excited about the test, to create a positive attitude toward testing, and to provide an excellent environment for test preparation in your home.

Brain research shows that students are better thinkers when they are not overwhelmed by stress. During testing periods, students must apply many, many thought processes using different parts of the brain. These connections are made more quickly and readily when the child's mind and body are relaxed. Anxiety, fear of failure, general stress, and negativity interfere with the ability to remember. By expressing pride in your child's hard work, confidence in his/her abilities, and a positive home environment for learning, you prepare your child's mind for tests and other learning experiences.

Test time is an exciting time for students. In class, I am helping your child develop confidence, improve memory, and learn strategies to do his or her best on the test. Thank you for participating in this effort at home.

When the test period is over, I will be hosting a class celebration. I hope you will be able to join us.

Sincerely,

_____ (teacher)

FIGURE 9.4

Test Talk

Negative Statements That Induce Stress

- I never did well on tests.

- I'll be extremely disappointed if you don't score high on the tests.

- Your brother never did well on tests.

- I hope your score is as high as your sister's score.

- You just don't do as well on tests as you do on other work.

Positive Statements to Encourage Test Success

- Give the test your best.

- Listen carefully and follow directions.

- The tests show how much you have stored in your brain.

- It's important to do your very best work.

- I will think about you during the test.

- The test will show us what you have learned.

- I will be proud of your hard work.

- You always do well on your work.

- Give it your best shot.

- Your teacher and I already know how smart you are.

- You have learned a lot.

- Have a great day!

- I love you!

FIGURE 9.5

Tips for Parents

➤ Be a cheerleader for your child's test success.

➤ Ease fears and anxieties.

➤ Identify self-defeating behaviors.

➤ Discuss the role of tests as one part of the total evaluation.

➤ Tell the child what to expect on the test.

➤ Talk about the value of good stress or the value of "butterflies in the stomach."

➤ Provide a good, nutritious breakfast.

➤ Be sure your child has a good night's rest.

➤ Emphasize the value of good nutrition and rest in learning and test success.

➤ Refer to the test as a special occasion to celebrate learning.

➤ Encourage your child to wear a favorite, comfortable outfit.

➤ Provide a relaxed, routine evening and morning before the test.

➤ Have an adventure with your child during the afternoon or early evening before the test.

➤ Celebrate learning when the test is completed.

THE TEACHER'S RESPONSIBILITIES

A large-scale process of change is slow, but you can improve the quality of your performance right away. All year, your approach and attitudes toward teaching shape the learning environment. On test day, your dress, body language, and degree of preparation communicate your expectations and attitude. Turning in a top performance is your responsibility.

Focus on Potential

Students thrive on challenges. Before each test begins, use empowering statements, such as "You are prepared for this test," "Remember your test-taking skills," "Pretend that you are solving a puzzle," and "I have confidence in you." When students are bored or feel defeated by unsuccessful attempts, their unchallenged, turned-off minds become sleeping brains. Too many times in testing experiences, students tune out and turn their brains off. It is the teacher's role to awaken their thinking minds and keep them fired up with confidence. This eliminates the mental shutdown. Allow students to be thinkers and problem solvers in learning adventures. Their minds and thoughts will come alive with ideas, thoughts, and creations. Students enter your room to see what you have to offer them. However, only students can control their own learning. When you teach the content information using a variety of effective strategies, you empower students to reach their learning potential during testing experiences.

A giraffe reaches and stretches its neck to the highest points in a tree, where it finds the greenest leaves to satisfy its hunger. It could find some leaves lower on the tree, but it thinks that reaching higher provides the best results. Plan daily lessons with opportunities for each student to reach high and explore ways to learn and retain information for test success.

Examine your own performance periodically using the Teach for High Achievement chart in Figure 9.6.

Teaching Test-Taking Skills

Teach test-taking skills throughout the year in innovative ways. Art Costa's (2007) model for teaching a thinking skill can be adapted and applied easily to teach a test-taking skill. Use the outline on page 204 of the Costa model as a guide to teach students how to transfer knowledge from prior experiences to the test format.

FIGURE 9.6

Teach for High Achievement

Teacher _____ Date _____

Rate yourself on your goals. Use the goals provided here or substitute some of your own. Place a checkmark in the appropriate column using the following scale:

1. Not Often   2. Sometimes   3. Often   4. Most of the Time

	1	2	3	4	Improvements Needed
1. I establish the concepts, goals, and objectives I am teaching.					
2. I vary instructional approaches because students learn differently.					
3. I teach for meaning and transfer.					
4. I believe my students can learn, retain, and use this information.					
5. I emphasize process over product.					
6. I use authentic assessment tools to assess learning.					
7. I establish a high-challenge environment.					
8. Students feel at home here.					
9. Students are excited about learning.					
10. I establish and enforce rules and guidelines.					
11. Materials and supplies are available and accessible.					
12. Students know their test-taking skills.					
13. Students know they can take risks.					
14. My students learn needed information and are able to transfer it to tests.					

FIGURE 9.7

Teaching a Thinking Skill	Teaching a Test-Taking Skill
I. Input • The skill or strategy is the lesson's focus. • It is taught in a variety of ways. • Students are told why the skill is important and when it will be needed. • Previous experiences are recalled. • The teacher or a skilled person models it. • Related vocabulary is introduced in each step. • Students discuss it.	• The test-taking skill or concept is taught explicitly. • The information is mentally processed in a variety of ways. • Prior experiences are woven into the lesson. • Use of the skill is modeled. • Vocabulary related to use of the skill is introduced. • Activities involve individual and group members in discussions of the skills used.
II. Process • The skill is experienced using known content. • The learners analyze their thinking about the skill in individual and group activities. • Sequential steps are used in applying the skill.	• The test-taking skill is applied with formal and informal tests using known content. • Students think about the test skill or strategy and verbalize their thinking during the experience. • When the information is processed, the learners talk out their thinking, step by step. They rehearse, analyze, and summarize the information to personalize the skill so it will be used automatically when needed.
III. Output • The skill is applied in new settings or contexts. • Students think about their thinking while completing each task to refine the skill's use. • The skill is applied in various ways in the classroom and in real-life situations.	• Learners apply and adapt the test-taking skill in a different way and often in a new topic, subject, or setting. • Students think about their use of the skill in formal and informal tests. • The information related to the skill's use becomes a part of each individual's repertoire of test application strategies.
IV. Reviews • Students review and apply each skill in future lessons and experiences throughout the year.	• The skill is used as needed in formal and informal tests to demonstrate ownership and understanding. • Chapter tests, unit tests, six-week tests, and informal tests offer opportunities for applying test skills and strategies.

Practice Sessions for Standardized Tests

Use the following approaches and suggestions throughout the year. These techniques are crucial for the students' test success.

Following Test Directions

Teacher's Role

- Use different tasks to perform in directions throughout the year.
- Teach the meaning of terms using words students understand.
- Create a research data wall of key words for instructions that is ongoing through the year. Ask students to display the word in a jazzy way on the wall with their interpretation of the action, the meaning, and an illustration. For example:
  - Word: Analyze
  - Interpretation of action and meaning: Dig deep, deep! (See "Sixteen Words for the Wise" in Chapman and King, in press [b], pp. 44–45.)
  - Illustration: A picture of something or someone digging
- Emphasize following directions in all activities and tests.

Test Taker's Role

- Read the directions carefully, word for word.
- Interpret the meaning of the key words in the instructions.
- Discover the instructed procedure expected.
- Follow the directions.

Answering Explicit Questions

Teacher's Role

- Model it! Share ways to approach and find answers to explicit questions.
- Teach this by asking students to point to explicit answers in the text.
- Use terms students can relate to, such as "Be a detective."
- Use tabbing, color coding, highlighting, and game formats to show students how to match each question with the answer.
- Practice throughout the year! Develop explicit questions using content information and facts about the students from their surveys. Practice until finding answers to explicit questions becomes an automatic skill for the test taker.

Test Taker's Role

- Discover what you need to find by reading the question thoroughly.
- Go into the paragraph and find the answer. Realize that you can usually put your finger on the answer to an explicit question.
- Mark the answer and move on to the next question.

Attacking Inference Questions

Teacher's Role

- Model and teach how to approach an inference question. Emphasize that these questions have answers hidden or not stated in the passage.
- Explain the difference between a detective and private detective. A detective finds the evidence that is at the scene, like an explicit answer, "It is right there." A private detective digs deeper and unlocks mysteries by finding the hidden evidence, like an inference answer.
- Realize that most inference questions are about the setting and the character.

  o Questions about the settings usually deal with the weather or the type of place in the passage.
  o Character questions deal with how the main character felt or how the other characters who were at the scene felt. The questions may refer to how characters would feel if placed in another time, such as today's world.
  o Use response cards to teach students to identify implicit questions.

    1. Make a response card for each student using a large index card.

    2. Draw a happy face, so-so face, and sad face vertically on one side of the index card. Draw the same faces on the other side of the card so all faces appear to be behind each other on the card.

    3. Read the implicit question and allow time for the students to select the answer.

    4. Say, "123, Show Me!" Everyone grasps or pinches the answer on the card between the thumb and index finger indicating the selected answer.

    5. Call on a student who has it right to share the answer. Then ask, "How do you know that?" or, "Why did you select that

one?" The student explains the discovery. When learners practice the skill throughout the year, inference questions on tests are easier. Always ask "why" or "how" questions until the students understand the approaches for answering inference questions.

Test Taker's Role

- Read the questions and all the possible answers.
- Identify an inference question by looking for the answer in the passage and discovering that it is not there.
- Know that most of the time, these implied questions are either about feelings of characters or settings.
- Become a private detective digging for the hidden mystery in inference questions. Realize that the answer is hidden in the paragraph.
- Find a possible answer and then ask yourself, "How do I know that?" When you can answer with accuracy based on what is written in the paragraph, you have found the right answer.
- Mark that answer and move on to the next question.

Unlocking Vocabulary and Meaning

Teacher's Role

- Set a goal for your students to broaden their vocabulary this year.
- Words and meanings are not mastered for long-term memory when they are taught in isolation. The saying "Use it or lose it!" applies to remembering words. Teach vocabulary words using them in content material and spiral the key words through conversations and daily lessons.
- Teach the meanings of words using age-appropriate wording instead of the definitions found in glossaries and dictionaries.
- Teach the meanings of suffixes and prefixes.
- Emphasize the meaning and the correct use of words more than correct spelling.
- Teach vocabulary skills in varied, unique ways.
- Celebrate when students use a more sophisticated word.

Test Taker's Role

1. Answer all questions you know first. Be careful to match the number on the answer grid with the number of the question.

2. Examine the unknown words in one of the following ways:

   a. Look for the base word.

   b. Identify the meaning of the prefix or suffix, if applicable.

   c. Interpret the meaning of the root word using its origin and meaning.

3. If you narrow the possible responses to two answers and you cannot decide which one is correct, select the one that feels "most right."

4. If you do not have a clue as to which response is correct, guess using your intuitive sense or first impulse. Be sure guessing does not count against you.

Solving Word Problems

Teacher's Role

- Teach the key words or phrases for the different operations. Develop a key category word list—for example, words and phrases used to add, subtract, multiply, or divide. Collect the words as they are taught or reviewed throughout the year. Challenge students to find the words to add to the list.
- Teach the step-by-step procedure and the thinking process for each operation. Remember, students must have time to process their thinking in order to be successful.
- Model the process for working various types of word problems using different operations throughout the year. After students solve a problem, give them time to talk to a partner or small group about the steps in the procedure or the process for solving the problem. Call on individuals to share their thinking with the class.
- Create a "Stretch Your Brain" station. Maintain this station throughout the year as a special place for students to write story problems. Use these student-generated story problems for bell-ringing activities, questions for games, or daily challenge assignments.

Test Taker's Role

1. Read the problem and look at the answer choices.

2. Identify the operation to use. Find key words that tell you what you are supposed to do and which operation you need to use to solve the problem.

3. Gather your data. Be accurate. Double-check your numbers.

4. Work each step of the process. Check to be sure you do not skip necessary steps.

5. Mark the answer and move on to the next question.

Completing Open-Ended Response Questions

Teacher's Role

- Teach students prewriting skills, showing them how to organize their thoughts.
- Remember these crucial facts to produce writers!
  - Students must write to learn to write.
  - Teach each skill with intriguing strategies.
  - Accept and praise efforts.
  - Teach students to say the information to themselves or to someone before they write. Ask students to memorize and use this statement: "If I can say it, I can write it!"
  - Emphasize the information more than spelling and other writing mechanics.
- Teach the content information before asking students to write about it. Remember, a student cannot write about an unfamiliar topic.
- Provide writing opportunities using different genres and topics.

Test Taker's Role

1. Read the question thoroughly. Decide what the author wants you to answer.

2. Say everything you know to yourself. Write it in a brainstorming list or plot the information on a graphic organizer.

3. Chunk or group the notes that go together.

4. Number the information in order.

5. Identify what goes in the main idea paragraph, the detail paragraphs, and how to restate the main idea in the closing paragraph.

6. Remember the purpose of writing is to get the information down to show what you know. Tell the information to yourself! Write it as you tell it. Do *not* skip a word. Use invented spelling.

7. If you get bogged down, refer to the notes and check them off as you use them.

8. Check to see that you have an opening and detail paragraphs with the main idea restated in the closing.

9. Read over your response. Add any part that was omitted. (See "Handy Dandy Essays" in Chapman and King, in press [b].)

Getting Your Act Together

Before the test, prepare yourself for your role as the testing director. Study the test guidelines and format thoroughly. Students will know when you are organized, and they will recognize your confidence. Know the step-by-step procedures and guidelines. Be sure the proctor, the students, and everyone involved understand and follow their roles.

Have test-related materials organized before the test, so you can concentrate on administering the test and meeting student needs. Follow the administrative guidelines and create a checklist similar to the one shown in Figure 9.8 to gather and organize the test materials.

FIGURE 9.8

Checklists of Materials for Tests

Teacher	Students
___1. Testing schedule	___1. Booklets
___2. Testing manual	___2. Answer sheets
___3. Directions for dispensing and collecting materials	___3. Scratch pads
	___4. Calculators
___4. Student materials and supplies	___5. Pencils with erasers
___5. Activities for stretch breaks	___6. Test survival kits
___6. Clock or timer	___7. Lucky Bucket
___7. Bottle of water	___8. Bottle of water

Testing Accommodations for the Special Needs Learner

Identify the student's needs and list adaptations required or recommended for testing. The student's individual education plan (IEP) often includes adaptations that must be in place for the learner. Adhere to all guidelines. Use the following suggestions when providing adaptations for students with special needs.

Before the Test

- Teach the information and skills using the learner's strengths in learning styles and intelligences.

- Introduce and model new skills or information using hands-on experiences or manipulatives.
- Rehearse the procedures in daily lessons.
- Wean students from adult dependence during independent assignments so they will be more self-directed.
- Teach and practice test-taking strategies throughout the year.
- Check for understanding by getting students to explain their thinking.
- Connect new skills and information to prior knowledge and/or meaningful experiences
- Conduct a conference with the student to discuss the upcoming testing event.

Preparing the Test Booklet

- Use larger print.
- Double-space the lines.
- Use symbols, colors, or unique designs to draw the learner's attention to specific functions, directions, or details.
- Highlight the important phrases and key words in the directions.
- Write lists vertically for easier reading.

Altering the Questions

- Use oral tests instead of written tests.
- Use simple words and phrases in the learner's language.
- Reduce the length of the passage the student needs to read or write to respond to the question.

Giving Directions

- Read directions aloud.
- Ask the learner to restate the directions.
- Make directions brief and clear.
- Rehearse the procedures in daily lessons.
- Give the student time to ask questions before beginning the test.

CURTAIN UP!

This book represents our vision of students preparing for tests through positive learning experiences. Just as you make a difference for learners in daily teaching, we want you to make a difference in their ability to succeed on tests now and throughout life.

In order for this to become a reality, the barriers to thinking need to be removed. Students need to know appropriate test-related behaviors, self-management techniques, rules, and procedures for tests. They need learning and transfer strategies that play to their strengths. For example, if a test calls for information learned through a rap, the student will be able to recall the words. If the information is learned through body movements, the student will be able to visualize the motions. If another student learned it through using a graphic organizer, that individual will be able to use the mind's eye to visualize the answer. When students are prepared as test-taking performers, they are ready to learn and to show what they know on test days.

The ultimate purpose of evaluation is to help students become independent learners.

We have raised the curtain for you by sharing our vision. The performance belongs to you, your cast, and your crew. As the pages of your curriculum unfold, we envision students who are challenged, retain more information, and enjoy learning. Our wish is that the skills and format of the standardized test are taught throughout the year. We hope each participant in the scene is prepared and the classroom is ready. Most of all, we hope you and your students have five-star testing performances!

Transform negative aspects of testing into positive learning experiences.

Embed test-taking skills in all curriculum areas throughout the year.

Spiral and integrate important skills across subject areas.

Teach and review content information using memory strategies.

Show students the many values of tests in school and in life.

Use testing data to design instruction for individual needs.

Customize test-taking experiences.

Create a positive test-taking climate throughout the school.

Enhance reviews using games, props, and rhythmic activities.

Share test preparation ideas with parents and the community.

Share your enthusiasm and celebrate learning.

Resources

Adapt the following form to assess those who play roles in your test-taking environment.

Roles for Testing	Strengths	Needed Improvement
1. Producer: Administrator		
2. Director: Teacher		
3. Eager Performer: Test Taker		
4. Prompter: Proctor		
5. Supporters: Other Staff Members		
6. Fans: Parents		

The following forms may be used to assess your own use of the many strategies presented in this book.

Chapter 4 Memory in Action	Page	Not Yet	Some	Often	Comments
1. Mnemonic Devices	36				
2. Visualization	37				
3. Imagery Slates	39				
4. Picture Organizers	42				
5. Basic Venn Diagram	43				
6. Thinking Boxes	47				
7. G. O. Dozen	47				
8. Color Coding	49				
9. Drawing Associations	49				
10. Acronyms	50				
11. Acrostics	51				
12. Rhyme It!	52				
13. Sing It!	52				
14. Rap It! Cheer It!	53				
15. Acting Out Concepts	54				
16. Chunking	58				
17. Categorizing	59				
18. Pegging	59				
19. Mind Joggers	60				
20. Memory Cues	61				

Chapter 5 Activities to Prepare the Test Taker	Page	Not Yet	Using	Comments
1. Brain Control—Teacher Script	66			
2. Wiggle Control	67			
3. The Brain at Work	67			
4. Brain Functions Chart	68–69			
5. My Great Brain Song	69			
6. Exploring Metaphors	70			
7. Egg Drop Contest	70			
8. Feeding Your Brain Chart	70–72			
9. Brain-Training Nutrition Checklist	72			
10. Testing, Testing! One, Two, Three!	74			
11. Standardized Testing Vocabulary Chart	75			
12. Physical Reactions to Test Stress Chart	76			
13. How to Overcome Fears Chart	78			
14. Relaxation Exercise: From the Deep	78			
15. Assessing Assessment Anxiety Chart	79			
16. Getting Yourself Ready: A Checklist	80			
17. Robot/Rag Doll Walk	81			

(Continued)

(Continued)

Chapter 5 *Activities to Prepare the Test Taker*	*Page*	*Not Yet*	*Using*	*Comments*
18. Confidence Indicator Checklist	82			
19. Dress for Test Success Chart	83			
20. Confidence Builders Checklist	84			
21. Conditions for Testing Comfort Chart	85			
22. Common Types of Distractions Chart	86			
23. Actions for Distractions Chart	87			
24. Desk Exercises	87–89			
25. Understanding Others' Needs	89			
26. Causes for Test Failure Chart	90			
27. Missed Shots	90			
28. How Much Will I Risk?	90			
29. Fishbowl Discussion Group	92			
30. How I Learn Best: Questionnaire	93			
31. Attitude Survey	94			
32. My Many Colored Days	95			
33. Posttest Feelings Questionnaire	95			
34. After-the-Test Self-Check Chart	96			
35. Action Lists Chart	97			
36. Good Test Behaviors List	97			
37. Ball Park View of Practicing: A Skit	98			

Chapter 5 *Activities to Prepare the Test Taker*	*Page*	*Not Yet*	*Using*	*Comments*
38. I Am Ready for the Big Test Song	100			
39. Testing and Maslow's Needs Hierarchy	101–102			

Chapter 6 Setting the Environment for Testing	Page	Not Yet	Getting There	Ready	Comments
1. Personalizing the Environment	106				
2. Seeing a Familiar Face	106				
3. Using Humor	107				
4. Removing Barriers	107				
5. Lighting	107				
6. Sounds	108				
7. Air Circulation	108				
8. Temperature	108				
9. Arranging the Scene	109				
10. Creating Privacy	109				
11. Creating Hype for the Production	110				
12. Sample Signs	110				
13. Sample Slogans	111				
14. Smiley Chain	111				
15. Genius Jar	111				
16. Brag Bag	112				
17. Cool Test Kit	112				
18. Cool School Tools	114				
19. Grand Openings	115				
20. Test Shower	115				
21. Cheers, Raps and Banner Themes	115				
21. Cross-Age Tutoring	115				
22. Prepare the School for the Performance	116				

Chapter 6 Setting the Environment for Testing	Page	Not Yet	Getting There	Ready	Comments
23. Decorated Door Celebrations	116				
24 Fanfares and Publicity	116				
25. Sing-Alongs	117				
26. Spirit Week	118				
27. Test Play	118				
28. Music Tests	119				
29. Library Tests	119				
30. Test-Ready Fling	119				
31. Sponsored Free Breakfast	119				
32. Parent-Sponsored Smart Carts	120				
33. Antics From the Principal	120				
34. Effective Transitions	120				
35. Letting Students React to the Test	121				
36. Quiet Time	121				
37. Cast Parties	122				
38. A Piece of Cake	122				
39. Energizing Cheers	122				
40. A Pat on the Back	122				
41. Whole-School Celebrations	123				
42. Teacher Performance Checklist	123				

Chapter 7 *Test-Taking Skills and Strategies*	*Page*	*Other Ways I Teach It*	*Not Yet*	*Mastered*
Tuning In ___ Reminder Jar ___ Directed Designs ___ Memory Tag ___ Ball Recall ___ Back to Back ___ Say It One Time ___ Orgami	 128 128 129 129 129 130 130			
Following Written Directions ___ Words in Action ___ Signs and Actions ___ React to the Facts ___ Step by Step ___ Mystery Numbers	131 131 131 132 132 132			
Bubbling In ___ Quick Activity Ideas ___ Mr. Bubble Cop ___ Perfect Penny Prints ___ Black Dot Mystery	 134 134 135 135			
Know and Go ___ Quick Pick ___ Base Race ___ Team Choice ___ Timed Games	 136 137 137 138			
Bee Back ___ Signal Time ___ Color Quest ___ Puzzle Play	 139 140 140			
When in Doubt, Try It Out! ___ Chain Links ___ Guesstimation Jar ___ Give It Your Best Shot! ___ On a Job Hunt	 142 142 142 143			

Take a Double Take! Check,
   Check!
___ Talk Your Thinking
___ Calculator Check
___ Journaling Activity:
   Mental Checks
	
	144
	144
	145			

Chapter 7 *Test-Taking Skills and Strategies*	*Page*	*Other Ways* *I Teach It*	*Not* *Yet*	*Mastered*
Set the Pace ___ Time Awareness ___ Pace Race ___ Pacing With the Animals ___ Discussion Prompts for Pacing ___ Color Coding the Speed Zones	146 146 147 147 147			
Keep On Keeping On! ___ Book Share ___ Piece by Piece ___ Interviews ___ Persuasive Selling ___ Come On Over to Our My Side	149 149 149 149 150			

Chapter 8 Attacking Passages and Solving Problems	Page	Other Ways I Teach It	Not Yet	Mastered
Attack Tactics for Multiple Choice Questions				
___ Scope It Out!	154			
___ Eye Spy	155			
___ Detective at Work	155			
___ The Game	156			
Responding to Open-Ended Test Questions				
___ The Great Eight	157			
___ The Writing Improve	159			
___ Direction Connection	160			
___ Direction Raps	160			
___ Word on Words: Test Terms	161			
Compare and Contrast				
___ Just Like Me	164			
___ Create a Venn Diagram	164			
___ Connection Blasts	165			
___ The Old Meets New	165			
___ Metaphor Mania	165			
Context Clues				
___ Thirteen Questions	167			
___ Spotlight Cues	168			
Cause and Effect				
___ Relationships in Math Chart	169			
___ Math Operations Chart	170			
___ Odd/Even Numbers Chart	170			
___ The Whys in My World	170			
___ If–Then	171			
___ Domino Effect	171			
___ Match Game Chart	171			
___ The Event From Both Sides	171			
Drawing Conclusions				
___ Footprint Hunt	173			
___ Target Practice	173			
___ Mystery Scenes	174			
___ Arrow Organizer	174			

Chapter 8 Attacking Passages and Solving Problems	Page	Other Ways I Teach It	Not Yet	Mastered
Fact Versus Opinion ___ Spider Organizer ___ Pet Facts and Opinions ___ Best of the Best ___ In the Game ___ Headliners With Facts and Opinion	175 176 176 177 177			
Zeroing in on the Facts by Scanning ___ Facts in the Spotlight ___ Facts in the Scene ___ The Eyewitness ___ Scanning Scavenger Hunts	178 178 179 179			
Getting the Point With Skimming ___ Table the Main Idea ___ Supporting Columns ___ Take a Peek ___ In the Headlines ___ Highlight Delight ___ The Skim Game	181 181 181 181 181 182			
First Things First: Using Sequencing ___ Tape Talk ___ Action Scenes ___ Sequence of Events for Test Day ___ Story Lines ___ The Times of My Life ___ Mimes in the Scene ___ Step by Step	183 184 184 184 185 185 185			

WE WISH YOU THE BEST FOR TEST SUCCESS!

References

Bruno, E. J. (1992). *The family encyclopedia of child psychology and development.* New York: Wiley.

Caine, R. N., Caine, G., McClintic, C., & Klimek, K. J. (2008). *12 Brain/mind learning principles in action: Developing executive functions of the human brain* (2nd ed.). Thousand Oaks, CA: Corwin Press.

Chapman, C. (1993). *If the shoe fits. . . . How to develop multiple intelligences in the classroom.* Thousand Oaks, CA: Corwin Press.

Chapman, C., & King, R. S. (2005). *Differentiated assessment strategies: One tool doesn't fit all.* Thousand Oaks, CA: Corwin Press.

Chapman, C., & King, R. S. (2008). *Differentiated instructional management: Work smarter, not harder.* Thousand Oaks, CA: Corwin Press.

Chapman, C., & King, R. S. (in press [a]). *Differentiated instructional strategies for reading in the content areas.* Thousand Oaks, CA: Corwin Press.

Chapman, C., & King, R. S. (in press [b]). *Differentiated instructional strategies for writing in the content areas.* Thousand Oaks, CA: Corwin Press.

Costa, A. (2007). *The school as a home for the mind: Creating mindful curriculum, instruction, and dialogue* (2nd ed.). Thousand Oaks, CA: Corwin Press.

Csikszentmihalyi, M. (1990). *Flow: The psychology of optimal experiences.* New York: HarperCollins.

Diamond, M., & Hopson, J. (1999). *Magic trees of the mind: How to nurture your child's intelligence, creativity, and healthy emotions from birth through adolescence.* New York: Plume/Penguin Group.

Gardner, H. (1983). *Frames of mind: The theory of multiple intelligences.* New York: Basic Books.

Gill, J. H. (1993). *Learning how to learn: Toward a philosophy of education.* Atlantic Highlands, NJ: Humanities Press.

Goleman, D. (2006). *Emotional intelligence: Why it can matter more than IQ* (10th anniversary ed.). New York: Bantam.

Gregorc, A. (2006). *The Mind Styles Model: Theory, principles, and practice.* Columbia, CT: Gregorc Associates.

Howard, P. (2000). *The owner's manual for the brain* (2nd ed.). Austin, TX: Bard Press.

Jensen, E. (2008). *Brain-based learning* (2nd ed.) Thousand Oaks, CA: Corwin Press.

Mentis, M., Dunn-Bernstein, M., & Mentis, M. (2008). *Mediated learning: Teaching tasks and tools to unlock cognitive potential* (2nd ed.). Thousand Oaks, CA: Corwin Press.

Nichols, S. L., & Berliner, D. C. (2008). Testing the joy out of learning. *Educational Leadership, 65*(6), 14–18.

Perkins, D. (1995). *Outsmarting IQ: The emerging science of learnable intelligence.* New York: Free Press.

Sousa, D. A. (2006). *How the brain learns* (3rd ed.). Thousand Oaks, CA: Corwin Press.

Sprenger, M. (1999). *Learning and memory: The brain in action.* Alexandria, VA: Association for Supervision and Curriculum Development.

Sprenger, M. (2006). *Memory 101 for educators.* Thousand Oaks, CA: Corwin Press.

Sternberg, R. J. (1996). *Successful intelligence: How practical and creative intelligence determine success in life.* New York: Simon and Schuster.

Sylwester, R. (2005). *How to explain a brain: An educator's handbook of brain terms and cognitive processes.* Thousand Oaks, CA: Corwin Press.

Turkington, C. (1996). *Twelve steps to a better memory.* New York: Simon & Schuster.

Index

CORWIN PRESS

The Corwin Press logo—a raven striding across an open book—represents the union of courage and learning. Corwin Press is committed to improving education for all learners by publishing books and other professional development resources for those serving the field of PreK–12 education. By providing practical, hands-on materials, Corwin Press continues to carry out the promise of its motto: **"Helping Educators Do Their Work Better."**